AFTER LIFE, THEN WHAT?

What to expect after death

Assure desired results

BY: DR. P. R. FROE

AFTER LIFE, THEN WHAT?

What to expect after death - Assure desired results

By: Dr. P. R. Froe

Copyright © 2018

Printed in the United States of America

First Printing, 2018

ISBN: 978-1-7327786-0-3

Lambs Great Commission
LambsGreatCommission@yahoo.com
http://www.LambsGreatCommission.com

Illustrations (Front cover page and Page 16) by:
Bidgie Froe © 2018

10 9 8 7 6 5 4 3 2 1

TABLE OF CONTENTS

AFTER LIFE, THEN WHAT?

DEDICATION TO DANA FROE

This book is dedicated to my beloved belated father, Dana Froe, who recently unexpectedly departed from this earthly realm. Although I have experienced materialistically loosing practically everything, the death of my dad was, by far, the greatest loss that I have ever suffered. I am now more sympathetic for those who were not raised by their dad. Since my dad was always present in my life (until recently), his being taken from me felt like someone ripped out an organ.

Prior to my dad's expiry, God graciously began preparing me for his passing, with the formulation of this book. During the creation of it, I thought that God was giving me revelation about death to edify the writing in this book. I know now that God was speaking to me in order to also prepare me for the coming of my dad's fatality. More importantly, I also immensely appreciate God for calling/bringing my dad into the Body of Christ before his demise. I thank God for the emotional and spiritual strength that I acquired while writing this book, which prevented me from feeling total devastation during my time of bereavement. And, similar to how the readers of the Book of Revelation are blessed, I pray a special blessing for all that read this book as well *(Rev 1:3)*.

INTRODUCTION

Planning one's path to financial success is common for many. People plan their short-term goals, mid-range goals, long-term goals, personal relationship goals, educational goals, business goals, etc. Contrarily, not many focus enough on spiritual goals or prepare well enough for their afterlife. This book deliberates on some of the most vital topics that have ever been discussed. And, if any of the readers have lost loved ones, as I have lost my father to death within a year of publishing this book, the contents of the book should strengthen them emotionally and spiritually, as it did for me. This book's material has been my comfort in my affliction. What God will do for one, He will do for others *(Rom 2:11)*.

According to Wikipedia encyclopedia, the **afterlife** (also referred to as **life after death** or the **hereafter**), is the concept of a realm, or the realm itself (physical or transcendental), in which a part of an individual's identity or consciousness, continues to exist after the death of their body/flesh at the end of the person's earthly life. The central aspect of the individual that lives on, after the death of the flesh, is believed to be a partial element of the earthly being (the soul and spirit of the individual). The soul and spirit contain the personal identity of that person. Since the afterlife is eternal and the human life is temporal or short-lived (typically 81 years or less), why wouldn't anyone prepare for the afterlife and set spiritual goals?

This book states why we all need to repent and submit to Jesus as Lord. Furthermore, it elucidates the afterlife benefits of Christianity and depicts the after death consequences of rejecting Jesus as Savior. The reading educates and encourages the reader's concerning the "Doctrine of Salvation" and "The Great Commission". It elaborates on the need for salvation and the process in which one can receive salvation. The contents of the book contains explanations and descriptions of various afterlife locations, redemption, God's end times timeline, grace, faith, justification, calling, election, predestination, foreknowledge, adoption, regeneration, propitiation, sanctification, glorification, preservation, salvation, spiritual growth, disciplines for maturity, sin, Bema Seat Judgement, Great White Throne Judgement, and more.

The book explains Christian responsibilities as a believer and addresses some of the most common Christian controversies (e.g. what happens after the 1st death, once saved ➜ always saved, predestination-election, free will of man, etc.). It may not resolve all Christian disputes regarding salvation; but, it should bring clarity concerning some of the most popular salvation related subjects. These writings teach why and how salvation is vitally necessary, and how one decision to accept or reject Jesus, will affect us eternally.

RESOURCE INFORMATION

A wide variety of media & sources (e.g. The Holy Bible, books, reports, internet, videos, sermons, interviews, articles, dictionaries, encyclopedias, commentaries, etc.) were used to acquire the necessary information in order to explain and advise believers concerning the above topics. Please note that all Scriptural references refer to the KJV Bible. The KJV of the Holy Bible is used because the NIV, NLT, NKJV, and ESV, etc., are **MISSING SCRIPTURES.** Yes, Scriptures have been taken out or removed.

Concerning the Holy Bible, beware that *Rev 22:18-19 (KJV)* states that "…If any man shall add unto these things, God shall add unto him the plagues that are written in this Book: And **if any man shall take away from the Words of the Book of this prophecy**, God shall take away his part out of the Lamb's Book of Life, and out of the holy city, and from the things which are written in this book".

MISSING BIBLICAL SCRIPTURES LISTING
Most Popular Bible Versions in Order of Popularity:

(1) **NIV** – (New International Version) - **Missing 16-Sixteen Scriptures**: i.e. *Matt. 17:21, 18:11, 23:14; Mark 7:16, 9:44, 9:46, 11:26, 15:28; Luke 17:36, 23:17; John 5:4; Acts 8:37, 15:34, 24:7, 28:29; and Rom. 16:24.*

(2) **KJV** – (King James Version) – **"NO" Missing Scriptures**

(3) **NLT** – (New Living Translation) – **Missing Scriptures**

(4) **NKJV** – (New King James Version) – **Missing Scriptures**

(5) **ESV** – (English Standard Version) – **Missing Scriptures**

Chapter 1

WHY DOES MAN NEED TO BE SAVED?

Death is a key reason why man needs to be saved.

A. *"The First Death" vs. "The Second Death"*

"The First Death" occurs when one's heart stops beating, their terrestrial flesh dies, and their human earthly life ends. This is a physical death. Know that death is NOT a total annihilation or extinction. The flesh of the person returns back to the dust from whence it came *(Job 34:15)*. The soul and the spirit of the person continue to exist. The spirit of the person goes back to God, who gave it *(Eccles. 12:7)*. Death is a separation. Man's flesh is separated from the soul and the spirit of that person. As we live from day to day, we continually come closer to our first death, when we disencumber our human flesh *(Heb. 9:27)*.

For Christians, the first death shall be as beautiful as a caterpillar (crawling wormlike creature) turning into a butterfly (flying, colorful, more-attractive insect). Solomon, who became king after David, was considered to be one of the wisest men of his time. In *Eccles. 7*, we learn from Solomon that **the end of a thing is better than the beginning of it**. Understand that when something is complete, it is better than it was at the time of its start. For example, when you have to cut your lawn, you may not want to do it, because you know that you will get tired and sweaty. The task requires energy and might be an unenjoyable chore. But after the task is complete, the lawn looks great, the person that cut the grass can rest, and they have not labored in vain. Likewise, after a believer experiences the first death, they can rest; their Christian labor was not in vain, and they will receive a glorified body (acquiring something more beautiful at the end than what they had at the beginning).

Unfortunately, for unbelievers, the death process will not be as wonderful. Those who reject Jesus as Lord will also experience **"The Second Death"** following the first death, which Christians do not undergo. The second death is spiritual and an eternally permanent separation from God *(Rev. 2:11, 20:6-14, 21:8; Jude 1:12)*. After the first death, unbelievers that have not accepted the Lord Jesus, await in hell for the second resurrection. After the second resurrection, they are judged at the Great White Throne Judgment for their sin. Afterward, they inherit the eternal Lake of Fire.

What happens to a person after they die (the first death) is determined by whether or not they have accepted God's offer of salvation. Salvation is deliverance from sin and its consequence (which is death). Salvation is acquired through repentance of one's sin in combination with believing that God raised Jesus from the dead, and accepting Jesus as Lord *(Luke 13:3; Rom. 10:9-10)*.

Salvation is an important subject to study due to man's original sin (also known as the "Original Fall" or "The Fall"). The fall of mankind caused a separation of man from God.

B. The Original Sin (a.k.a. The Fall of Man) and God's Saving Grace

Even before God the Father sent His Son, Jesus, to earth to reconcile man from sin, He continuously displayed His grace by repeatedly saving people from danger and destruction *(Gen. 19:19, 50:20, 45:7; Exod. 14:13, 15:2)*. From the beginning, God has continually proven that He can deliver us when no one else is capable of doing so. Sometimes, nothing less than a miracle can help our situations. Jehovah God is the ultimate omnipotent (all-powerful) Savior, who is able to save us from anything *(Matt. 14:30; Jer. 42:11; 2 Kings 19:34; Dan. 6:27; Heb. 11:7; 2 Pet. 2:5)*. God's saving grace is essential for humanity due to "Man's fall."[32]

We can learn about the "Fall of Man" from the Book of *Genesis* in the Holy Bible. In Genesis, we discover that before Eve was created, God instructed Adam not to eat from the tree of the knowledge of good and evil *(Gen. 2:17)*. God warned Adam that if he disobeyed the command and ate fruit from that tree, he would surely die. Adam refrained from sin prior to God giving instruction regarding the tree of good and evil. But Adam was created as a free-will agent (just as all men are) with the capability to sin. While Adam remained obedient to God, he was in perfect fellowship with Him. During the period when man had a faultless fellowship with God, He proclaimed that it was not good for man to be alone *(Gen. 2:18)*. To resolve this, God created a woman from the rib of Adam for his companionship.

The woman was named "Eve." Adam and Eve lived in good standing with God until Satan, in the form of a serpent, tempted Eve to eat fruit from the tree, which God had forbidden *(Gen. 3)*. The serpent was more cunning and clever than any other animal of the field. His intention was to cause the fall of man just as he had fallen out of fellowship with God.[30]

C. Satan's Fall from Heaven to Earth

Initially, Satan was named Lucifer, meaning the bright one, "the son of the morning." Lucifer was created as a beautiful cherub or angel, and he was covered with precious stones *(Ezek. 28:12-17)*. After Lucifer attempted to take over God's throne, he lost his favor with God *(Luke 10)*. He was then called Satan and cast out of heaven. He desired to replace the most-high God, Jehovah, and also attempted to set up his own throne so that he could be worshipped.

Instead, as a result of his jealousy and pride, he shall be brought down to hell and cast into the lake of fire *(Rev. 20:14)*. Satan led a rebellion in heaven against God before his fall and persuaded other angels to follow him. He was successful in beguiling approximately one-third of the angels in heaven to turn against God *(Matt. 12:24; 2 Pet. 2:4; Rev. 12:4)*. Satan's defiance against God, caused him to fall from heaven like lightning *(Luke 10:18)*.[30]

D. The Gap Theory – Between Gen 1:1-Gen 1:2

"Gap theory" believers conclude that Satan's fall took place after *Gen. 1:1*, and before *Gen. 1:2*. The Gap theory is a controversial topic. Some place a gap of an indeterminate amount of time between the first two verses of *Gen. 1*.

> *Gen. 1:1-2* = *In the beginning God created the heaven and the earth. And the earth was without form, and void; and darkness was upon the face of the deep. And the Spirit of God moved upon the face of the waters.*

Controversy over what happened during the gap period exists amongst the gap theory believers. Most versions of the gap theory will place millions of years of geologic time between *Gen. 1:1* and *Gen. 1:2* (using justification including billions of fossil animals). This is called the "ruin-reconstruction gap theory." This theory contradicts Holy Scripture because it would mean that death, bloodshed, and disease existed before Adam's sin or the "Fall of Man." We must not allow fallible scientific theories determine Scriptural interpretations.[31]

Some assume that the fall of Satan occurred within the gap period. However, the rebellion of Satan during the gap period contradicts God's description of His completed creation on the sixth day, when He describes everything as being "very good" *(Gen. 1:31)*. When considering the points that are made by gap theory believers versus those who oppose the gap theory, one should keep in mind that the Bible simply does not validate the occurrence of the gap theory.

Since God does not elaborate on the original creation and destruction of the earth in Scripture, we should not allow different unproven scenarios or speculation to cause division amongst believers.[31]

E. Satan's Temptations

Satan has continued to tempt mankind into disobeying God, since the beginning *(Gen. 3:1-5).* He tempted Eve when he asked, "Hath God not said, ye shall not eat of every tree of the garden?" Satan's question caused Eve to second-guess God's instructions. Eve responded by informing Satan that God has allowed Adam and her to eat of all the trees of the garden except the one tree that is called the tree of the knowledge of good and evil. She also mentioned that they could not even touch the tree lest they die. Satan, the father of lies, tells Eve that she would not SURELY die if she were to consume fruits from the forbidden tree *(John 8:44).* Satan beguiled Eve into believing that God withheld information from Adam and her *(1 Tim. 2:14)*, and that if they ate of the fruit of the tree, they would learn hidden truth, becoming like God.[31]

F. How Did Eve React to Satan's Temptation?

Initially, Eve conceived the fruit to be good for food, and it appealed to her fleshly senses. The beauty of the fruit appealed to her emotions, and the thought of obtaining the knowledge of God appealed to her intellect. This was very similar to how Satan also tempted Jesus *(Luke 4:1-13).*

Today, Satan continues to deceive man with temptations that appeal to weaknesses of the flesh, emotions, and intellect.

Eve, who was created to be a helpmeet for Adam, began to doubt God regarding the forbidden tree. She also failed with regard to her responsibility as Adam's helper. Eve decided to disobey God before consulting Adam. Then, she tempted Adam and convinced him to also disobey God by eating of the forbidden fruit. Sin and rebellion appear to be contagious by nature and do not remain limited to the original sinner.

Adam was not deceived by the serpent according to *1 Tim. 2:14*. He must have eaten the forbidden fruit because of his love for Eve. Adam chose death with Eve over life without her. Although Eve was the initial transgressor and was the first to sin, Scripture places the guilt on Adam *(Rom. 5:12-18; 1 Cor. 15:22)*. Adam was the head of his relationship with his wife, Eve. Therefore, God initially gave the command regarding the forbidden tree of life to him, not Eve. [31]

G. Adam and Eve Become Ashamed

The eyes of Adam and Eve were opened after their consumption of the forbidden fruit. As a result of this unveiling, they saw themselves to be naked, and they were ashamed *(Gen. 3:7)*. So, they attempted to cover their nakedness using fig leaves. Humans have been covering nakedness ever since. What is worse, the couple's sin broke their fellowship with God. The penalty of sin is death, and the effect of sin is separation from God because God must be separated from sin *(Gen. 3:8-24)*.[31]

Since God created us and sustains us, he has the right to establish laws that His creation should obey regardless of whether or not we understand why He created the regulations. God's laws are spiritual, as well as material. We must trust that God had man's best interest at heart when establishing His laws. Humans need God's laws, which provide guidance when men exercise their free-will. Unlike God, man is not omniscient (all-knowing). God does not treat humans like puppets on a string. He does provide us with the necessary guidance and direction to make the right decisions in life if we submit to His authority.[31]

Adam and Eve became sinners from disobeying God and could not elude the presence of God because God is omnipresent (God is everywhere). After Adam sinned, God called for him. Adam was afraid and knew that he was naked, so Adam hid *(Gen. 3:10).* The holiness of God exposes our sin. God asked Adam and Eve about their disobedience and how they knew that they were naked. They both tried to justify their transgression by passing the blame. Adam told God that the woman that He had given him encouraged him to eat (blaming Eve and God). Eve responds by saying how the

serpent beguiled her (blaming Satan). *[See: Gen. 3:11-13]*
We must not follow this example of passing the blame when
we are confronted about our sins. Instead, we should confess,
repent, ask for forgiveness, and attempt to sin no more *(1 John
1:9; James 5:16; Luke 13:5; Rev. 2:5)*. The way to get God's
forgiveness is through confession of our sins rather than
denial. All who desire Jesus as their Lord must confess their
sin, accept the responsibility for their actions, repent, and
acknowledge the need for God's grace and mercy. [31]

H. Judgment of Adam, Eve, and Serpent - Their Sin Penalty

Man must take responsibility for their actions according
to God's law, and God must judge transgression from His
laws. God's judgment on the serpent for his part in the fall of
man resulted in the serpent being cursed above all cattle and
above every beast of the field. The serpent was made to go
upon its belly and eat dust all the days of its life. God also put
mutual hatred between it and Eve, and between its seed and
her seed *(Gen. 3:14-15)*. Additionally, God's judgment, or
the effects of man's sin, affected all of the animal kingdom
(Jer. 12:4; Rom. 8:20). [30]

God's punishment for Eve and all women thereafter,
was that their sorrow in conception would be more severe
(Gen. 3:16). The wives' desire would be to the husband, and
the husbands shall rule over their wives. Nevertheless, today,

women continue to rebel against God's rules of authority and continue attempting to rule over their husbands/men. [32]

Mankind was punished by having to labor continuously and work more strenuously. They are to have greater professional hardships, more difficulty providing for their families, and more challenges with their financial endeavors *(Gen. 3:17-19).* Not only must men now work harder, but they must return to the dust from which they were formed, experiencing physical death or the first death *(Eccles. 3:20).*[32]

I. *Atonement or Covering of Man's Sin*

"Atonement" of sin is a "covering" and reconciliation of God with humans brought about by the redemptive life, sacrificial death, and the resurrection of Jesus, the Christ. Atonement is God's display of grace and Him making a provision for man's sin. Christ shed His blood when He died on the cross at Mount Calvary, in order to atone for the sins of all mankind because the penalty of sin is death *(Rom. 6:23).* Therefore, He offered His own life and died for man's sins so that we may have eternal life. The life of Jesus was not taken from Him on the cross; instead, He laid it down Himself for mankind *(John 10:17-18).* By doing so, Jesus gave humanity a second chance to receive eternal life and avoid eternal damnation.

Although man had forsaken God, God will never leave or forsake His children *(Heb. 13:5)*. All that repent and accept Jesus as Lord by faith, will not experience the "second" death, which is eternal separation from God in the "Lake of Fire" *(1 Thess. 4:16)*. Man's sin causes separation from God. And it is due to the gift of salvation that man can be reconciled back to God. Sin is universal. All humans are born in terrestrial bodies of flesh that are incapable of living perfectly sinless. Man, by his own actions, can NOT be redeemed from sin. And the consequence of man's sin is separation from God, which is death.[2]

For this reason, man needs salvation more than anything else (more than money, cars, fame, relationships, and any other materials that this world can offer). The "Good News" is that God offers this salvation through His Son, Jesus. This "Good News" is the main revelation of the Holy Bible. The Book of *Genesis* teaches us about man's need for salvation because of sin. The Book of *Revelation* is the total fruition of salvation and is recognized with the prophecy of the creation of a new heaven and a new earth *(Rev. 21:1)*. This book provides a functional and practical understanding of the afterlife/salvation and deals with the more essential elements related to this subject. The Writings are specifically written for this current historical end-time season.

J. Theology - Christian Soteriology

The term "Theology" was derived from two Greek words (from Greek Θεός meaning "God" and λογία, -logy, meaning "study of"). Theology is the systematic and rational study of God's concepts, their influences, and the nature of religious truths. Theology can also refer to the learned profession that is acquired by completing specialized training in religious studies at places such as a university, school of divinity, or seminary.[1]

In theology, the study of salvation is called "Soteriology." The term "**Soteriology**" is derived from the Greek σωτηρία / *sōtēria* / *sōtērion* (meaning "salvation") and from σωτήρ / *sōtēr* (meaning "savior, redeemer, or preserver") and λόγος *logos* "study" or "word" (and the English word "logy"). Soteriology is the study of religious doctrines of salvation.

K. Salvation - Restoration - Deliverance

Salvation relates to restoration, deliverance, and redemption, and includes a past, present, and future tense. Once we repent, accept Jesus the Christ as our personal Lord and Savior by the confession of our mouths, and believe in our hearts that God has raised Him from the dead, we are considered to be saved "Christians" or "Born-again Believers" *(Rom. 10:9-10; Luke 13:3)*. Believers are saved, restored, and delivered from the second death which is the penalty of sin

(Rom. 6:23). In other words, through our faith in Christ, we are saved from eternal damnation and instead inherit eternal life. Salvation is God delivering believers in Christ from the bondage of sin and condemnation. As a result of the atoning sacrifice of Jesus, when He gave His life on Mount Calvary for the remission of man's sin *(John 10:18)*, Christians will receive eternal life and God's Kingdom of Heaven *(Col. 1:13)*.[4]

According to *Eph. 2:8*, we are saved by grace through faith as a gift of God; and not of ourselves. Some present this idea as initial, progressive, and final salvation.

L. Initial, Progressive, and Final Salvation

"Initial Salvation" refers to the time when a person repents from their sin, professes Jesus to be their personal Lord and Savior, and believes that God raised Him from the dead *(Rom. 10:9-13)*. As a result, they receive God's forgiveness for their sins and His gift of salvation. At this point, they go from a state of spiritual death to eternal life, from darkness to light, and from the power of Satan to the power of God *(John 5:24; Acts 26:18; 1 John 3:14)*. According to Scripture, they become free from the slavery of sin and are considered by God to be His righteous sons *(John 8:32-36; Gal. 3:26; Rom. 3:22, 6:22)*. Understand that God saves us because He is merciful, not as a result of our righteous works. In His grace, God saves us by spiritual renewal and the infilling of the Holy Spirit. We are justified by God's grace so that we are saved *(Titus 3:4-7)*.[1]

"Progressive salvation" refers to the course of a person from the time of their spiritual conversion until their physical death. This is the path of their eternal life, which they travel with faith in Jesus and the power of the Holy Spirit *(Gal. 3:2-5; Rom. 8, 6:20-23)*. During this progressive period, they strive for peace and holiness while the Holy Spirit sustains them *(Heb. 12:1; 1 John 1:9; 1 Cor. 1:7-9)*. [1]

"Final salvation" refers to the entrance into God's kingdom for those who are made righteous by God after they experience physical death. Final salvation relates to the event of God saving those (who have accepted Jesus as their Lord) at the final judgment. There is a great divide between believers and non-believers. Believers are united with Christ by their faith in the Lord and are accepted by God on the grounds of their submission to Jesus. Understand that even after receiving the gift of eternal life, one is also still on the road that leads to eternal life *(Matt. 7:14, 25:46)*. I say this because after one receives eternal life through belief and confession of Jesus as Lord, they still possess a "free-will" that allows them an option of straying from God, falling away from their faith *(2 Thess. 2:3)*, and even turning from God as Satan has done *(1 Tim.*

6:10, 5:15, 21; 2 Tim. 2:18; 2 Pet. 2:15; Luke 8:13; Matt. 11:6, 26:31). In fact, turning away from the Lord may seem common during the time of the prophesized great apostasy or the end-time falling away, because many will choose not to resist Satan's influential temptations *(Matt. 24:10; 2 Thess. 2:3; 1 Tim. 4:1; 2 Tim. 4:4).* But if we resist the devil, he will flee *(James 4:7).*[1]

Chapter 2

SALVATION IN BIBLICAL SCRIPTURE

In order to understand the meaning of eternal life-salvation and the requirements of it, we need to be aware of what God's Scripture teaches us about it. Salvation is a major topic in Scripture, so let us consider the following Scriptures that are related to the Good News of Salvation:

For God so loved the world, that he gave his only Son, that whoever believes in him should not perish but have eternal life (John 3:16; see also John 5:24; Acts 2:21; Rom. 5:8, 10:13, 8:32; I John 5:13). Nothing will separate God's children from His love *(Rom. 8:35-39).* According to *Mark 16:16, whoever believes and is baptized will be saved, but whoever does not believe will be condemned (Rom. 8:1; John 20:31).* This does not mean that baptism is mandatory for salvation (See: Chapter-7/Section-E = *Once You Have Answered the Call, Is Water Baptism Required for*

Salvation?). Those that do not obey Jesus shall not see life, and the wrath of God remains on him *(John 3:36)*. However, when God grants one eternal life, they will never perish *(John 10:28)*.

> *1 John 5:11-13* = *And this is the record, that God hath given to us eternal life, and this life is in his Son. He that hath the Son hath life; and he that hath not the Son of God hath not life. These things have I written unto you that believe on the name of the Son of God; that ye may know that ye have eternal life, and that ye may believe on the name of the Son of God.*

By God's grace, we are saved through faith. Salvation is a free gift from God and is not a result of our own works, so that no one may boast *(Eph. 2:8-9)*. Developing our relationship with God is an important part of Christianity. Even though we live during the "Grace Dispensation" and not under the "Dispensation of the Law," keeping God's commandments, is an indication that we know Him. Whoever does not keep His commandments, yet says that they know Him, is a liar failing to be honest *(1 John 2:3-4, 5:1-5)*. Jesus is considered to be the Shephard of His flock or His sheep (Christians). These sheep hear His voice. He knows them, and they follow Him. Jesus gives them eternal life, and they shall never perish *(John 10:27-30)*.

Understand that we must choose salvation. God has created us in His image as free-will beings, and He allows us to decide for ourselves whom we shall serve *(Josh. 24:15)*. Humans were created to worship and serve God. If one declines to worship or serve the one and only Holy God, they **will** worship or serve something or someone in place of God (whether they deliberately attempt to or not). It is in man's nature to worship, and when man fails to worship God, Satan is glorified.

Becoming a born-again Christian is a great way to begin planning your afterlife. When people identify themselves as "saved Christians," they are professing that they are believers in Christ, who are saved from damnation and the Lake of Fire, by God's grace and the blood sacrifice of Jesus. Salvation is the saving of one's soul from the second death, which is the result of, or the penalty for, sin *(Rom. 6:23)*. Salvation is also referred to as "Redemption" or "Deliverance" from sin. All men have sinned because all humans are born with a natural sin proclivity *(Rom. 3:23)*. For this reason, ALL are in need of justification, sanctification, and glorification.

If someone has truly made Jesus the Lord of their life, they can be certain of their salvation *(Rom. 10:9-10; Acts 16:31)*. The Holy Spirit bears witness that we are children of God *(Rom. 8:16; John 1:12)*. God instructs us to repent and be baptized in the name of Jesus Christ for the forgiveness of our sins, and we will receive the gift of the Holy Spirit *(Acts 2:38-39; 1 Pet. 3:18-22)*. There is no other name by which man can be saved except Jesus Christ *(Acts 4:12)*. Jesus declared that He is the way, the truth, and the life. No one goes to the Father God, Jehovah, except through Him *(John 14:6)*. Receiving the gift of the Holy Spirit is being born-again of the Spirit. Jesus professed that unless one is born of the Spirit, they cannot see the kingdom of God. One must be born of water and of the Spirit because that which is born of the flesh is flesh, and that which is born of the Spirit is spirit *(John 3:1-5)*. Everyone who has been born-again of God overcomes the world and its problems, by their faith *(1 John 5:4-8; John 3:3)*.

Christians are required to love our brothers; whoever does not love abides in death *(1 John 3:14, 4:21, 5:1)*. If any man says that they love God and hate their brother, he is a liar *(1 John 4:20)*. How can anyone NOT love their brother whom they have seen, and claim to love God, whom they have not seen?

Born-again Christians are not to make a practice of sinning because the Holy Spirit dwells within them, and they cannot continue to sin without chastisement from God, which causes remorse that leads to confession/repentance *(1 John 3:9)*. If one is without chastisement by God, then they are bastards, and not sons of God *(Heb. 12:6-8)*. Christians may not be perfect when it comes to sin abstinence, but they develop habits of righteousness. Whoever does not practice righteousness is NOT of God *(1 John 3:10)*.

Once a person is in Christ, they become a new creation, and the old person passes away *(2 Cor. 5:17)*. The new man has the help of the Holy Spirit, which keeps us from being drawn to sin if we resist. Because we are still human, we may still sin. Know that our omniscient God is aware of all of our sins; yet, He still requires us to confess our sins. If we confess our sins, God is faithful and just to forgive us of our sins and to cleanse us from all unrighteousness *(1 John 1:9)*. We must examine and test ourselves to see whether or not we are in the faith, and to consider our works for the Lord *(2 Cor. 11:28, 13:5)*.

Although we are not saved by our works, God will render to each person according to his works, whether they be good works or bad works *(Rom. 2:6-8)*. We must do the will of our Heavenly Father *(Eph. 2:10)*. Not everyone who says, "Lord, Lord," will enter the kingdom of heaven; they must do the will of God the Father *(Matt. 7:21)*. Many will assume that because they prophesied in the name of Jesus, cast out devils, or did many other wonderful works, that they will inherit the kingdom of God. And God will profess unto them,

"I never knew you, depart from me, ye that work iniquity" *(Matt. 7:22-23)*.

It is not God's desire to reject any from His kingdom inheritance. This is why He is patient towards us. God wishes that none should perish, but that all should reach a point of repentance *(2 Pet. 3:9)*. Without confession/repentance, our sins are not redeemed/forgiven, and a separation from God results. Contrariwise, the free gift of God is eternal life through Jesus *(Rom. 6:-23)*.

Pray that God delivers you from evil. Jesus teaches us how to pray for deliverance in *Matt. 6:9-13*. We should immediately pray after all transgression because tomorrow is not promised to us. Today could be our last day and our last opportunity to confess/repent. Everybody will die once, and after that comes judgment *(Heb. 9:27)*. We must remain Christ-like and remember Him in everything that we do *(1 Cor. 11:1-2)*.

Christians are to trust in the Lord and lean not to their own understanding *(Ps. 37:5; Jer. 17:7-8; Prov. 3:5)*. Our trust in the Lord triggers peace with God through Jesus *(Rom. 5:1)*. (See also: *Eph. 1:4; 2:5; 1 John 2:15, 27, 3:18-24, 2:27, 5:16-17; James 2:14-26; Hebrews 10:10 & 21-23; 1 Cor. 11:27-30; Rom. 3:10, 23, 4:25; John 20:19-23; 2 Thess. 3:6; John 8:31-32; 1 John 1:8; 2 Peter 1:10; John 6:54, 15:8; Luke 8:13.*)

Chapter 3

AFTERLIFE LOCATIONS

A. Sheol, Hades, Abraham's Bosom, The Pit, and The Grave

One of the most significant reasons that man **needs** salvation is to avoid eternal damnation and the "Lake of Fire." Hell, also known as Sheol, or Hades, is taken from the English word from a Teutonic root meaning "to hide" or "cover."[2]

"Sheol" is a Hebrew term that refers to a temporary address of the disembodied souls of the dead. The word Sheol is used interchangeably with the Greek word **"Hades."** Before the resurrection of Christ, both the souls of the evil and the righteous went there after death. Scripture refers to it thirty-one times as **"The Grave,"** thirty-one times as **"Hell,"** and three times as the **"Pit."** Sheol (or Hades) has two separate halves or portions. One side is a place where the unbelieving evil are tormented. The other side is called **"Abraham's Bosom,"** according to *Luke 16:22*. Abraham's

Bosom was the place of comfort and rest for the righteous *(Luke 16, 23)*. There is an impassable canyon or gulf that divides the two halves.

After Christ was resurrected, numerous Old Testament saints were resurrected and were seen by many *(Matt. 27:51-53)*. Sheol (or "Hades") is described as being "*in the heart of the earth*" based on *Matt. 12:40* and is thought to be below, down, or beneath in passages such as *(Deut. 32:22; Isa. 14:9; Ezek. 31:16)*.

In some Scripture, "Sheol" and "Hades" are translated as **"Grave,"** but the grave is only the place for the body after death, not the place for the soul. This could cause confusion when certain verses refer to a righteous man going to "Sheol," such as men like Jacob and Joseph, *(Gen. 37:35; Job 14:13)*. These men did not go to the place of torment. They went to the comforting side of Sheol (Hades), called Abraham's Bosom.[9&34]

The Greek word "**Hades**" is also called "Sheol" (Hebrew). It is not the grave or sepulcher, nor is it the eternal location of the souls of the dead. Hades is the place for the soul of a person and not their body.[34]

B. Gehenna and Hell

The word "**Gehenna**" is Greek, but is originally from the Hebrew name **Gehinnom**. The terms were derived from the **Valley of the Son of Hinnom,** which was known in the Hebrew Bible as a place south of ancient Jerusalem. The Valley of Hinnom surrounds Jerusalem's Old City and merges into the Kidron Valley near the southeastern corner of the city.[2]

According to the Hebrew Bible, some of the kings of Judah sacrificed their children by fire in Gehenna, which is why it was deemed to be cursed *(Jer. 7:31, 19:2-6)*. Gehenna is a destination of the wicked and a permanent place for the destruction of their soul and body. It is a place where the worms do not die, and the fire is never quenched *(Mark 9:45)*. Those who enter Gehenna, do so as body and soul. Many have concluded that it occurs after the resurrection of the unbelieving damned at the time of the Great White Throne Judgment.

Gehenna is the **"Lake of Fire,"** which is described in *Rev. 19, 20*. It is presently uninhabited, but the Beast and the False Prophet will be cast into it at the end of the tribulation phase *(Rev. 19:20)*. After the one-thousand year reign of Jesus, Satan and the unbelievers of all previous time periods will be cast into the Lake of Fire *(Rev. 20:10-15)*. They will all burn in Gehenna, or the Lake of Fire, together eternally. Hades and Gehenna are not the same places *(Rev. 20)*. At the Great White Throne Judgment, which is at the end of the one-thousand year millennial kingdom of Christ, those in Hades will be removed (**Rev. 20:13** - ". . . *HELL* [Hades] *delivered up the dead which were in them . . .*"). And those unbelievers, which were in Hades, will be cast into the Lake of Fire or Gehenna, after their Great White Throne Judgment **(Rev. 20:14-15).** [2&34]

  Rev. 21:1 says, "*And I saw a new heaven and a new earth: for the first heaven and* **the first earth were passed away**; *and there was no more sea.*" Hades, which will be emptied **(Rev. 20:13)**, will ultimately be destroyed since it is in the heart of the first earth or the center of the first earth. The Valley of Hinnom was a place where the bodies of dead animals and rubbish were taken to be burned, and it symbolizes the future destruction of the wicked in Gehenna. The Valley of Hinnom was also where human sacrifices were made unto the pagan false god, Molech **(2 Kings 23:10; 2 Chron. 28:3, 33:6; Jer. 32:35).** [9&34]

Jer. 7:31-32 = "*And they have built the high places of* **Tophet**, *which is in the* **valley of the son of Hinnom**, *to* **burn their sons and their daughters in the fire**; *which I commanded them not, neither came it into my heart. Therefore, behold, the days come, saith the LORD, that it shall no more be called Tophet, nor the valley of the son of Hinnom, but the valley of slaughter: for they shall bury in Tophet, till there be no place.*"

Hence, the Valley of Hinnom is a place called "Tophet" whose name means "place of fire".

The Greek word **"limne pur,"** also known as the "Gehenna" or the "lake of fire," occurs four times in the Holy Bible *(Rev. 19, 20).* This is the place where the unbelievers are casts and eternally tormented. "Limne" also can be interpreted as "lake" and is translated like this in all ten of the times that it occurs in the KJV Holy Bible. The word "Pur" is translated as "fire" and is translated as such seventy-three times by the KJV, and it is translated as "fiery" once.[34]

C. *Tartarus*

"Tartaroo" (Greek) refers to "Tartarus" and occurs only once in the KJV of the Holy Bible in *2 Pet. 2:4,* where it is translated as "hell" (*"For if God spared not the angels that sinned, but cast them down to **hell**, and delivered them into chains of darkness, to be reserved unto judgment . . ."*). This is likely a lower place in hell which is separated from the other parts. Some suspect that this may be a place only for fallen angels *(see also Jude 1:6).*

In Greek mythology, the fallen angels or giants are referred to as "Titans," and Tartarus is the thought to be the deep abyss that is used as a place of torment, imprisonment, punishment, and suffering for the disobedient, wicked Titans. Tartarus was also imagined by those who believe the Greek mythology to be a primeval force or deity.

The English word "**Grave**" is an unearthing or excavation for the interment of a corpse or a place of burial. This is the place for someone's fleshly body to be put after death. It is a sepulcher or a burial vault. It is NOT the dwelling place for the soul (the mind, emotions, and will) or the spirit of the deceased person.[9&34]

D. The Abyss, Chasma, and Paradise

The Greek word "**Abussos**" is also known as the "**Abyss**" and is translated in the KJV of the Holy Bible as "bottomless pit" five times, "deep" twice, and "bottomless" twice. This is the place where Satan will be locked up for the 1,000 years during Christ's reign on earth after His second coming *(Rev. 20:1-3)*. In *Luke 8:30-31*, we learn that a legion of devils begged Jesus not to send them to the abyss, or the bottomless pit, that will be opened at the fifth trumpet judgment according to *Rev. 9:1-11*. There will be a beast that will come out of it at the fifth trumpet. *(See also: Rev. 11:7, 17:8)*. Some think that the Abyss is the same as the impassable gulf that is described in *Luke 16:26*. This place is also known as a "**Chasma**" (Greek), which is a gaping opening, chasm, or gulf. It is translated "gulf" in its one and only Biblical occurrence in *Luke 16:26*, where it is the canyon that separates the torment side from the comfort side of Hades.[23&34]

"Abraham's Bosom" that is mentioned in *Luke 16:22*, is known as "**Abraam kolpos**" in the Greek language. The "Bosom of Abraham" is a place in Sheol where the dead righteous are comforted. We find that Abraam is translated "Abraham" seventy-three times. The word "Kolpos" was translated into "bosom" five times and "creek" only once *(Acts 27:39).*

"Paradeisos" is translated "paradise" three times by the KJV. In *Luke 23:42-43,* we find out about the communication between the thief and Jesus on their crosses. The thief asked Jesus to remember him when Jesus enters His kingdom. And Jesus told him that **"To day"** he would be with Him in Paradise. Remember that Jesus was not resurrected until 3-three days after His death. Additionally, Paul tells us in *2 Cor. 12:4* that he was he was caught up into Paradise where he heard unspeakable words that are not lawful for humans to speak. Moreover, in *Rev. 2:7*, Jesus let the church of Ephesus know that those who overcome (staying grounded in their faith), will be allowed by Him to eat from the tree of life that is found in the midst of God's Paradise.

The tree of life is also mentioned in *Rev. 22:2*, in the new heaven and new earth. Evidently, there will be more than one tree of knowledge during this era. There will be multiples of a type of life tree. The three Scripture references show paradise to be in different places. Therefore, some believe that paradise is relocated, while others think that the word "paradise" is just a general term.[9&34]

To avoid confusion, one should be careful when using the word "**Hell**" because it is translated from different words in the Bible. It is translated in the Old Testament from the words "Sheol" or the (Pit/Grave) and in the New Testament as "**Gehenna**" or "a place of burning." Hell is also translated once from the Greek word "tartaroo or a place of darkness *(2 Pet. 2:4)*", and "hades or the abode of the dead (the grave)."

Hell is referred to as a place of punishment for the unbelieving lost or unrepentant. Scripture indicates that it is a place where the wicked are tormented *(Luke 16:23)*. Hell is described not only as a place of eternal fiery torment, but it is a place where worms don't die *(Mark 9:41-48)*. Note that worms scavenge dead flesh and are mentioned doing so in several places in Scripture, such as *Job 21:26* and *Isa. 14:11.*

According to *Rev. 14:9-11*, the third angel will say with a loud voice, "if any man worship the beast and his image, and receive his mark in his forehead, or in his hand, the same shall drink of the wine of the wrath of God, which is poured out without mixture into the cup of his indignation; and he shall be tormented with fire and brimstone in the presence of the holy angels and in the presence of the Lamb.' The smoke of their torment will ascend up forever. And they have no rest day or night, who worship the beast and his image, and whosoever receives the mark of his name. The "mark of his name" is "the mark of the beast" – *(Rev. 9-11)*.[9&34]

E. Lake of Fire

The eternal **"Lake of Fire"** is worse than hell. This fiery lake will be a place where eternal torment is experienced constantly day and night. The names of those who confess Jesus as Lord are written in what is called, "the Lambs Book of Life" *(John 3:3-7)*. This book contains the names of those who shall be saved or spared from eternal damnation in the lake of fire. Whoever's name is not found written in the book of life shall be cast into the lake of fire.

Rev. 21:8 warns that those who are fearful, unbelieving, abominable, murderers, whoremongers, sorcerers, idolaters, and all liars, shall experience the second death and burn in the lake, which burns with fire and brimstone *(*see also: *1 Cor. 6:9-10; Gal. 5:19-21; Col. 3:5; Eph. 5:5)*. Additionally, one must be willing to forgive others of their trespasses in order to be forgiven by our heavenly Father, so that they may evade the lake of fire *(Matt. 6:14-15, 18:22-35)*.[34]

Christians must endure to the end, maintaining our faith in Jesus or continuing to believe, in order to stay clear of the fiery lake *(Matt. 10:22; John 6:66-67)*. One must not turn from God when we are tested in our trials, during persecution, or throughout tribulation *(Luke 6:22, 8:13; 2 Tim. 3:12; John 15:20; Matt. 13:21)*. Unfortunately, all who start with Jesus will not remain with Him because they may afterward be swayed to believe in false teachings of cults or false religious sects, etc.

(See: 1 John 2:24-25; 2 John 9; Gal. 5:2-4; 1 Cor. 15:1-2)

Those that claim that they believe in Christ, but don't produce fruit, are in danger of the Lake of Fire; because if one abides in God, and He in them, they will bring forth much fruit *(Matt. 25:14-46; John 15:5-6).*

If a former Christian (one who did NOT remain faithful to Jesus) receives the mark of the beast and worships his image, they, too, shall inherit the lake of fire *(Rev. 14:9-12, 13:8-10).* Those that perform un-repented gross immorality, injustice, or wickedness are also in danger of the hellfire.

> *Matt. 13:41-42 = The Son of man shall send forth his angels, and they shall gather out of his kingdom all things that offend, and them which do iniquity; And shall cast them into a furnace of fire: there shall be wailing and gnashing of teeth.*

F. Paradise vs. the Heaven(s)

First, know that man's imagination is not broad enough to totally comprehend all of the divine truths about "Paradise" or the "Heaven(s)." Hence, God does not Biblically tell us everything about them. However, He does give us some explanation of them in Scripture.

"Paradise" is a place of contentment, happiness, delight, and fulfillment. It is sometimes referred to as a higher place or the holiest place, unlike "hell" or the "underworld." The Abrahamic faiths associates paradise with the Garden of Eden prior to man's original fall from God's grace. From an eschatological perspective, there is also a paradise that is thought to be the abode of the Godly believing dead, which is located below the surface of the earth.[2&5]

"Heaven" is described by Wikipedia to be a higher place, a paradise, or the holiest place, which is distinctive from "hell" or the "underworld." The Old Testament in the original Hebrew language used the word "heavens" rather than "heaven." The Bible actually describes three different heavens. The **"first heaven"** is the firmament or sky that covers the earth *(Gen. 1:8)*. This is the realm of the birds and clouds that surrounds the world. It is the atmosphere or what is above the surface of the earth *(Gen. 1)*. The **"second heaven"** is the physical universe where the stars, sun, moon, planets, and galaxies dwell *(Exod. 32:13)*. It is referred to as the "outer space." This is the space that is beyond the earth, and it covers the universe. It is located as far as human eyes can see with a telescope. The **"third heaven"** is unseen and is the abode or residence of God and Jesus. Beasts sing continually declaring, "Holy, Holy, Holy, Lord God, Almighty," over God's mercy seat or throne *(Rev. 4:8-11)*.[2&5]

  After Christ's return, God provides a new heaven and a new earth. The first heaven and the first earth will pass away. And there will be no more sea. The apostle John also tells us that a New Jerusalem will descend out of heaven, coming down to earth *(Rev. 21:1-2)*. This New Jerusalem will be the tabernacle of God or the dwelling place of God. The tabernacle will be with men. There will be righteousness and no more death, sorrow, crying, or pain *(Rev. 21:3-4)*. This city will not have a need for the sun or the moon to shine on it, because God's glory will provide the light *(Rev. 21:23)*. Only believers, those whose names are found in the Lamb's Book of Life, will be allowed in this city *(Rev. 21:27)*.

  Jesus assured us, that in the Father's house are many mansions, and that He will prepare a place for believers *(John 14:2)*. Therefore, do not store up treasures on this earth. Moths/rust can destroy earthly treasures or thieves can steal them. There are better reasons, to earn heavenly treasures. Your heart is found where your treasure is *(Matt. 6:19-21)*. Some say, that you can tell how much one loves God by analyzing, how they use their time and how they spend their money.[2&5]

Chapter 4

REDEMPTION OF MANKIND

"**REDEMPTION**" signifies the buying back of something or someone that is lost, alienated, or mortgaged. Redemption involves paying a price to return something to your possession. It means to buy out and may denote the deliverance from danger, violence, or oppression. It can apply to a person's life and relates to laws. Redemption is the action of saving or being saved from man's sin, error, or evil. It is the regaining or gaining possession of something in exchange for a payment or the clearing of a debt. It refers to retrieval, recovery, reclamation, repossession, returning, exchange, cashing in, conversion, paying off, discharge, clearing, honoring, fulfillment, carrying out discharge, performing, and/or the action of buying one's freedom. God desires that all mankind be redeemed.[33]

A. Redemption in the Greek

Redemption is the English translation of the Greek word "AGORAZO," meaning "to purchase in the marketplace." In ancient times, it often referred to the act of buying a slave. Christians use the term "Redemption" to mean that Jesus Christ, through His sacrificial death, purchased believers from the slavery of sin to set us free from that bondage and offer mankind a second chance to receive eternal life with God.[1&23] "EXAGORAZO" is another Greek word relating to this term.

Redemption involves going from something to something else. Jesus frees man from the bondage of the law to freedom of a new life through Him. The third Greek word connected with redemption is "LUTROO," meaning "to obtain release by the payment of a price." The blood of Christ that was shed when He died on the cross at Mount Calvary is the payment that obtains our release from the bondage of sin. [23]

The Israelites were redeemed from Egypt. We were redeemed from the power of sin and the curse of the Law *(Gal. 3:13)* through Jesus the Christ, our Redeemer *(Rom. 3:24 & Col. 1:14)*. Man was bought with the price of His death *(1 Cor. 6:20, 7:23)*.

B. Our Faith is Redeeming

Redemption is Christ's resolution of the penalty of man's sin that allows man to be reconciled back to Jehovah God. Man's liability to the punishment of sin was destroyed, and man, through his faith in Christ and acceptance of Jesus as Lord, can receive eternal life in God's kingdom. Man now has an option to elect receipt of God's gift of faith, as the means to their inheritance as a child of God.[33]

C. Covenant Theology

(Redemption-Works-Grace Covenants)

The "Covenant of Redemption" is one of the three theological covenants. The three theological covenants of covenant theology are:

1.   The Covenant of Redemption
2.   The Covenant of Works
3.   The Covenant of Grace

The **"Covenant of Redemption"** refers to the covenant within the Trinity Godhead (Jehovah God the Father, Jesus Christ the Son, and the Holy Spirit/Holy Ghost), which establishes the plan of salvation. That is the agreement within the Godhead that the Father would appoint the Son to give up his life for mankind and that Jesus does it *(Titus 1:1-3).* It is called the Covenant of Redemption, yet some think that the wording is inappropriate for the following reasons:

1. They attest that the two sides of a covenant are not usually equal. The covenant is established by a sovereign person with a lesser person. In the Old Testament, Kings made a covenant with a nation that he defeated. A covenant is believed to be like a bond in blood that is supremely administered. Since the persons of the Trinity are equal, there is no one particular sovereignty in this Agreement of Redemption.

2. Covenants were instituted by blood, which was to be an indication of what would happen to the person who would break the covenant terms. Covenants and testaments differ. A testament is established by law when the person dies. On the other hand, in a covenant, the person can die if they fail to uphold the terms of the covenant. The Agreement of Redemption was for Jesus to die even though it was man that sinned (NOT Jesus).

3. Some covenants are made due to the possibility of one of the parties violating the terms of the agreement. The covenant holds the parties accountable. The agreement of redemption did not have the potential to fail. On occasion, it is referred to as the "Intra-Trinitarian Covenant."

Redemption (during life, at death, and after death) is a subject that Christian churches have disagreed on throughout history. Paul uses the idea of redemption to acknowledge the saving consequence of the death of Christ. In *Exod. 21:8*, redemption referred to the ransom of slaves. In the New Testament, redemption is used to refer both to deliverance from sin and freedom from captivity. Redemption is a metaphor for what is accomplished by the atonement. Jesus paid the price of a ransom with His life, which causes Christians to be released from the bondage of sin and death. Many evangelical theologians and Protestant denominations do NOT believe that the ransom price of redemption was paid by God to Satan.[33]

Luke 27-28 informs us that there will come a time when Jesus will come back in a cloud with power and great glory. When this comes to pass, we are advised to stand up and lift our heads, because redemption is drawing near. No man lives without sin. All have sinned and are justified freely by God's grace through the redemption that came by Christ Jesus *(Rom. 3:23-24)*. By the blood of Christ, we are redeemed and forgiven of our iniquity and bequeathed with God's grace that He gave us with wisdom and understanding *(Eph. 1:7-8)*. Christ redeemed us from the curse of the law by becoming a curse for us (being hung on a cross that was made of tree wood). It is written: "Cursed is everyone who is hung on a tree" *(Gal. 3:13)*.[33]

Man needs to acknowledge, turn from, and feel regret for his sin in order to receive God's gift of redemption. *Luke 13:3 – I tell you, Nay: but, except ye repent, ye shall all likewise perish. (See also: Mark 7:8-9, 20-23)* All men are born sinners as a result of "The Fall" of Adam and Eve *(Rom 3:23; Rom 5:12).* Therefore, ALL need to repent.

We may find ourselves guilty of sins of "omission" as well as sins of "commission." Sins of commission are wrongdoings against God's will, statute, or instructions. The sin of omission is failing to do what God desires us to do. Confession and repentance are needed regardless of the type of sin that we are found guilty of. All sin is sin, whose penalty is death, and the gift of God is eternal life through Jesus Christ our Lord *(Rom. 6:23)*.[33]

The **"Covenant of Works"** is the second of the three theological covenants and the pre-Fall agreement between God and Adam. Adam was promised blessings and life as long as he was obedient to the terms of the covenant. He was also warned about the cursing and death that would occur if he became disobedient to the terms of the covenant.

The **"Covenant of Grace"** is the last of the three theological covenants of Covenant theology. This third Covenant of Grace promised eternal blessing for the belief in

Christ and obedience to God's Word. It's the foundation for all biblical covenants that God made individually with Noah, Abraham, David, Israel, and with man in the New Covenant.

Chapter 5

GOD'S BENEVOLENT GRACE

"Grace" is defined as "the love and mercy of God" that is given to us because God wants us to have it. We can NOT earn it, nor do we deserve it. Grace is God's unmerited favor that our actions do not warrant. It is kindness and compassion from God that we are not worthy of. It is a gift. Grace is divine assistance given to humans for their regeneration (rebirth) or sanctification. It is a state of sanctification and consecration through God's divine kindness.[19] Grace can be explained with the following acronym:

God's
Riches
At
Christ's
Expense

Grace is God's generous superior assistance that He gives us. God's grace is a free gift that was initiated by Him and may take the form of divine favor, love, clemency, and kindness. It is an attribute of God and is manifested in the salvation of sinful humans that would have been damned eternally without it.[33]

The question of the means of grace is controversial. The Roman Catholic Church holds that grace is infused in a particular way (not only one way) by the reception of the sacraments that confer the gifts of God, which include faith. Many Protestants believe that Grace is given by God based on the faith of the believer, which is also a gift from God.

> **Eph. 2:8** = *For by grace you have been saved through faith, and that not of yourselves; it is the gift of God.*

Lutherans attest that grace is "the Gospel in Word and sacraments." The sacraments are means of grace that includes the teaching of John Wesley. Arminians understand the grace of God to be one's cooperating with their free-will for salvation. They appear to have an assumption about the abilities of man to decide his salvation apart from God's grace. The Church of Christ believes that the grace of God that saves man is the plan of salvation. They see the plan for salvation differing from salvation itself. The plan for salvation involves the following two parts:

1) The perfect life, death, burial, and resurrection of Jesus the Christ

2) The Gospel, New Testament, or the faith

The ***Book of James*** distinguishes between a dead faith (a faith without works) and a living faith (a faith accompanied with works of obedience). God's gift works through a person's faith resulting in salvation.

A. *How the Bible Describes God's Grace*

1. The Law of Moses contrasts grace *(Rom. 6:14; Heb. 10:4; John 1:17)*. Paul's contrasts between work and faith, as well as the works of the Old Covenant and obedient faith under the New Covenant.

2. Grace saves and justifies *(Ro. 3:24; Ti. 3:7; Eph. 2:5)*.

3. Grace can't be added to *(Gal. 5:4)*.

4. Grace teaches and can be preached *(Ti. 2:11; Eph. 3:8)*.

5. Grace calls us *(2 Tim. 1:9 & Gal. 1:15)*.

6. Grace is brought by revelation *(1 Pet. 1:13)*.

7. Grace and truth came through Jesus Christ *(John 1:17)*.

8. Grace is sufficient for us *(2 Cor. 12:9)*.

The thought of God's grace brings peace. In ***Titus 2:11,*** Paul uses the expression "*the grace of God*" to refer to the Savior of mankind. The phrase "the grace of God" can be used interchangeably as a synonym for Jesus. "The goodness of God" and "the loving-kindness of God" are seen through

Jesus and His works *(see: Titus 2:11, 3:4-6).* Jesus experienced death for mankind so that we would have a second chance to receive eternal life and avoid the second death *(Titus 2:9).* [21&27]

Jesus is full of grace and truth and is a reflection of God's favor *(John 1:14).* Unlike man, Jesus did not allow distractions to interrupt His fellowship with God the Father. Jesus set an incredible example for us and exhibited faultless obedience despite the adversary's temptations to sin. John acknowledged Jesus' fullness and grace in *John 1:16-17.*

John 1:16-17 = *And of his fulness have all we received, and grace for grace. For the law was given by Moses, but grace and truth came by Jesus Christ.*

"Grace for grace" means that Grace is interchanging with grace. Grace was replaced by more grace or greater grace. By God's grace, we are offered an opportunity to experience an improved spiritual relationship and fellowship with Him. We can encounter greater spiritual understanding and strength, as well as God's favor. Grace is given in proportion to our spiritual growth, which comes because of God's fullness. [21]

The "Church of Christ" believes that God's grace provides the following PLAN, which results in salvation:

- One must hear the Gospel/Word *(Rom. 10:17).*
- Believe the Gospel *(Mark 16:15-16).*
- Repent of sins *(Acts 2:38).*
- Confess their faith in Christ as Lord before men *(Matt. 10:32; Rom. 10:9-10).*
- Be immersed into water in Christ for the remission of sins *(1 Pet. 3:21; Rom. 6:3-18; John 3:3-5; 1 John 5:6-8; Acts 2:38; Mark 16:16.)*
- Live faithfully even to the point of death *(Rev. 2:10; Rom. 11:17-22; James 5:19-20).*

Have you ever received a gift that you did not deserve from someone that loves you? If so, God's grace should be easier to understand. Grace is God showing His love to you even though you don't deserve it and can't earn it. God shows believers grace by sparing us from the penalty of sin (the second death/the lake of fire). Through His grace, He gives us strength, guidance, and protection.

> ***Eph. 2:8*** *= For by grace are ye saved through faith; and that not of yourselves: it is the gift of God:*

As we freely receive God's grace, we should freely give grace to others – *(Matt. 10:8).*

Chapter 6

THE NECESSITY OF FAITH

According to TheFreeDictionary.com, **"FAITH"** is strong or unshakeable belief in something, especially without proof or evidence. It is a specific system of religious beliefs. Christians trust in God, His promises, and actions. Others have developed acceptance of numerous firmly held principles or belief systems, in which they have placed allegiance or loyalty to. Bad faith usually relates to insincerity or dishonesty. Good faith is associated with honesty or sincerity. The Wikipedia Dictionary defines "FAITH" as a confident belief in the truth, value, or trustworthiness of a person, idea, or thing. It is a belief that does not rest on logical proof or material evidence, but rather involves trust instead. It involves loyalty to a person or thing and is an allegiance. Christian faith is considered to be the theology that is defined as a secure belief in Jehovah God and a trusting acceptance of His will.[2&6]

Heb. 11 informs us that faith is the substance of things hoped for and the evidence of things not seen. Through faith, we understand that the world was built by the Word of God. We see that the faith of Abel offered a better sacrifice unto God than that of Cain. Noah displays his faith when he created the ark after being warned by God of things that were difficult to believe without faith. His faith saved his family.

By faith, Abraham went to a place where God sent him to receive an inheritance. He abided in the land of promise dwelling in tabernacles with Isaac and Jacob. Abraham looked for a city that would have foundations, whose builder and maker was God. Due to Sarah's faith, she conceived a child after she passed the childbearing years. [21]

Faith is a miraculous gift from God *(1 Cor. 12:9)* and a characteristic that man willingly receives. When one has faith, it exists in their mind and heart. It is a response to the Holy Spirit's influence. God can NOT believe or have faith for man. It is one's own mind and being that believes *(2 Thess. 3:2)*. Faith comes from hearing, and hearing comes from the Word of God *(Rom. 10:17)*. Paul understood that faith is built and developed; it grows, deepens, and enlarges. He encouraged believers to increase their faith or allow their faith in God to grow. *2 Thess. 1:3 - We are bound to thank God always for you, brethren, as it is meet, because your FAITH GROWETH EXCEEDINGLY, and the charity of every one of you all toward each other aboundeth.* Soundness of faith results from hearing, thinking, learning, and trusting. It may also follow victory after rebuke *(Titus 1:13).* [33]

A. Faith is Needed for Salvation

Salvation is not a reward for our good works. We are saved by grace if we have faith in Jesus, who died for our redemption. This faith allows us to submit to Christ in acceptance of Him as Lord. Mankind was justly condemned to death for sin and disobedience due to the original fall of man. As a result of that initial fall of Adam and Eve, all men are born into sin and have no standing before God in their own righteousness. Inasmuch as *"there is none righteous, no, not one,"* all need God's grace and favor *(Rom. 3:10).* We are made righteous through Christ by His righteousness *(Rom. 5:19).* [33]

God made the first move to rescue humanity from the damnation of sin. After the fall, God made efforts to reconcile all men back to Himself and recover mankind from Satan's influence. God is pleased with those who accept His offer by confessing their faith in Jesus. Those who respond to God's offer of His Son to become our Lord and Savior are blessed with eternal life and an inheritance in heaven. [33]

The word 'grace' is first used in Scripture in regard to Noah *(Gen. 6:8 - "But Noah found grace in the eyes of the LORD.")* The faith of Noah in God saved him and his family from death in the flood. And now that Jesus has laid down His human life in sacrifice as an atonement for man's sin, those with faith in our Redeemer will eternally commune with God. Faith makes old things pass away and all things become new *(2 Cor. 5:18).* Those believers who were once far from God are brought nigh or close. They pass from death to an everlasting life and from disobedience into son-ship. They move from evil doers with fleshly desires to men of good works and Godly spiritual fellowship. They change from sinners facing damnation, into children of God that receive a priceless eternal life. The Apostle Paul describes these changes in *(Eph. 2:1-13).*[33]

(Eph. 2:1-13) = *And you hath he quickened, who were dead in trespasses and sins; Wherein in time past ye walked according to the course of this world, according to the prince of the power of the air, the spirit that now worketh in the children of disobedience: Among whom also we all had our conversation in times past in the lusts of our flesh, fulfilling the desires of the flesh and of the mind; and were by nature the children of wrath, even as others. But God, who is rich in mercy, for his great love wherewith he loved us, Even when we were dead in sins, hath quickened us together with Christ, (by grace ye are saved;) And hath raised us up together, and made us sit together in heavenly places in Christ Jesus: That in the ages to come he might shew the exceeding riches of his grace in his kindness toward us through Christ Jesus. For by*

*grace are ye saved through faith; and that not of yourselves: it
is the gift of God: Not of works, lest any man should boast.
For we are his workmanship, created in Christ Jesus unto
good works, which God hath before ordained that we should
walk in them. Wherefore remember, that ye being in time past
Gentiles in the flesh, who are called Uncircumcision by that
which is called the Circumcision in the flesh made by hands;
That at that time ye were without Christ, being aliens from the
commonwealth of Israel, and strangers from the covenants of
promise, having no hope, and without God in the world: But
now in Christ Jesus ye who sometimes were far off are made
nigh by the blood of Christ.*

B. Faith and the Road to Salvation

Recognizing God's blessing helps us to comprehend
His goodness. This brings us to admittance, confession, and
repentance of our sins. After learning of the blessing of Christ
at the cross, if we believe in Jesus as Lord, we will be saved
(Acts 16:31). Jesus purchased mankind with the fatal shedding
of His own blood at Calvary. Salvation is a free gift that is
offered to any person that receives Jesus as their Lord in faith.
All devoted believers have the authority to speak on behalf of
Christ.

The **"Great Commission"** of the believers is to lead
the lost unbelievers to our Lord, Jesus, for reconciliation and
salvation. It is a command that comes from Jesus Himself,
directing believers to spread the Gospel to all nations *(Matt.
28:19-20)*. Jesus explained how salvation comes through faith.
Man is saved by grace, through faith, and through believing

the Word of Truth (remember that Jesus is the Word made into Flesh). God's loving grace and mercy is the "Good News" message of promise that requires nothing more than faith *(Isa. 55:1-3)*.

Once we make a faith decision, we can learn to love God because He loved us first *(1 John 4:19)*. Subsequently, we begin to love other Christ minded believers more. And during this spiritual growth, our compassion begins to grow also for those who lack faith (as Christ demonstrates compassion to all).

Chapter 7

JUSTIFICATION EXPLANATION

The Doctrine of Justification in Christian theology is God's act of removing the guilt and penalty of man's sin and simultaneously making sinners righteous through Christ's atoning sacrifice of Himself on Mount Calvary's cross. God acquits the sinner and considers that sinner to be forgiven. Righteousness comes from God and is accredited to the sinner through their faith and acceptance of Jesus as Lord [not by the good works of man]. There is a three-phase plan for salvation where Jesus saved us from (1) the penalty of sin, (2) the power of sin, and (3) the presence of sin. The penalty or wages of sin is death. The power of sin is the flesh (our terrestrial bodies). The presence of sin is found on earth and in this world.[33]

Our being saved from the penalty of sin is called "**JUSTIFICATION**," which is in the past tense *(Eph. 2:8-9 - For by grace are ye saved through faith; and that not of yourselves: it is the gift of God: Not of works, lest any man* *should boast)*. Our being saved from the power of sin is called "**SANCTIFICATION**," which is in the present tense *(Phil. 2:12 - Wherefore, my beloved, as ye have always obeyed, not as in my presence only, but now much more in my absence, work out your own salvation with fear and trembling)*.

Our being saved from the presence of sin is called "**GLORIFICATION**," which is in the future tense *(Rom. 13:11 - And that, knowing the time, that now it is high time to awake out of sleep: for now is our salvation nearer than when we believed)*. We have been saved. We are being saved. And we will be saved.[29]

This whole three-phase plan of salvation is called "**RECONCILIATION**." Reconciliation is where our perfect God brings sinful mankind back to Himself. Justification is to be made righteous, just, holy, and acceptable before God. It is being changed from the "state of sin" to the "state of grace." When we are in the state of sin, we alienate ourselves from God, and there are no good works that man is capable of doing that would earn or merit our own justification. The grace and justification that God allows us to experience are free. The word "grace" comes from a Greek word meaning "favor" or "gift."[29]

Paul tells us that "justification" comes through faith or by faith. Our belief needs to go hand in hand, or in conjunction with submission to God/Jesus/Holy Spirit. St.

James teaches that even the satanic demons believe. Still, they do not submit to God; therefore, their belief does not bring them God's grace. James informs us how there is only one true God that causes even demons to tremble with fear because they not only believe in God's existence, but they know His power *(James 2:19)*. We need to have repentant faith in order to receive God's justification *(Luke 24:47; Acts 2:38, 3:19, 17:30; Rom. 2:4; 1 Cor. 7:9-10)*. Demons lack sorrow for their sin. They do not wish to change or turn from their wicked ways. Repentant faith leads to justification and includes hope for God's mercy.[29]

Paul's teaching concerning justification by faith (not works) must be considered in conjunction with other Biblical passages that speak about the sacramental aspect of justification. Paul does not regard Baptism as one of the human "works of the law." Baptism is a work of God that is a display of our obedience to the instructions of Jesus.

> *Matt. 28:18-20* = *And Jesus came and spake unto them, saying, all power is given unto me in heaven and in earth. Go ye therefore, and teach all nations, **baptizing them** in the name of the Father, and of the Son, and of the Holy Ghost: Teaching them to observe all things whatsoever I have commanded you: and, lo, I am with you always, even unto the end of the world. Amen.*

Water Baptism displays participation in the death of Christ. By this sacrament, we receive the grace that Jesus won on the Cross by His death. The resurrection of Christ enables us to live an eternal life *(Rom. 6:3-4)*. Paul spoke about the role that Baptism plays. Paul recalled Ananias encouraging people to be baptized to wash away their sins *(Acts 22:16)*. The baptism that saves you now is by the Holy Spirit and not the cleansing from physical dirt, but it is a commitment to God through the resurrection of Christ for those who fall from grace because of sin. This sacrament is necessary *(John 20:22-23)*.[29]

The Protestant Reformation began when Luther, a Catholic monk, rediscovered a Catholic justification by faith doctrine in a Catholic book. The "Reformation Doctrine of Justification by Faith" is the main target of the enemy's attack because it is the foundation of what reconciles God and man. Therefore, Satan has caused many to exchange Godly Biblical purity for entertainment that pleases the flesh and/or motivational speeches. Theologically, justification describes what God proclaims believers to be, NOT what He does to change believers. Justification does not change the sinning believer's nature or character. It is a divine judicial edict. Justification only changes our status with God. However, behavioral changes will take place afterward.[29]

Biblically, justification is a divine verdict that finds a sinner "not guilty and fully righteous." Humankind was formerly condemned, and now, they are vindicated. Sinners who once lived facing God's wrath convert to believers that are now under God's blessing. Justification is even more than a pardon. A pardon would leave the sinner without merit in God's sight.

God imputes righteousness to the sinners when He justifies them *(Rom. 4:22-25, 5:19; 1 Cor. 1:30; Phil. 3:9).* Through Jesus, justification frees believers from guilt and accredits merit to their personal account *(Rom. 8:33, 5:17).* Furthermore, it allows us to become adopted children of God and fellow heirs with Jesus, our Redeemer *(Rom. 8:15-17).*[29]

A. Justification Differs from Sanctification

God does not justify sinners according to their good works of the law. He justifies sinners by their faith in Jesus Christ *(Rom. 3:28; Gal. 2:16).* "Justification" imputes Christ's righteousness to the sinner's account *(Rom. 4:11),* and "Sanctification" imparts righteousness to the sinner's personally *(Rom. 6:1-7, 8:11-14).* To be sanctified is to be made holy. God officially accepts and approves the person. "Justification" takes place outside the sinner and changes their standing *(Rom. 5:1-2),* and "Sanctification" is internal and changes the believer's state *(Rom. 6:19).* "Justification" is an event; whereas, "Sanctification" is a process.[29]

God does not justify those whom He does not sanctify and vice versa. "Justification" and "Sanctification" are both necessary for salvation. One needs to have clarity about how they differ. The differences between the two were one of the main issues between Rome and the Reformers in the sixteenth century.[29]

B. Justification through Christ

There are three classes of relations in the Gospel (i.e. governmental, spiritual, and those that unite both of these). Currently, Jesus provides our justification. Justification is not the Law pronouncing the sinner to be just. It is the sinner being governmentally treated as if he were just. It involves a governmental decree of pardon or amnesty (where the penalty of the law is not suffered). The sinner is restored to be favored and rewarded as if they had been righteous.

The Old Testament practices of sacrifices taught us that the doctrine of pardon is built on the basis of faith, repentance, and atonement. This was under the old dispensation of the law and is represented as a merciful acceptance of sorrowful remorse. The mercy-seat shielded the two tablets of the Law (a.k.a. the Ten Commandments) that were in the Ark of the Covenant. (Note: The Mercy Seat was the golden lid or cover that was placed on the top of the Ark of the Covenant, in the

Holy of Holies, and behind the veil *(Exod. 26:34, 30:6)*, where the presence of the Lord was manifested *(Lev. 16:2)*.[29]

Rom. 4:6-8 = *Even also as David describeth the blessedness of the man to whom God imputeth righteousness without works, saying, blessed are they whose iniquities are forgiven, and whose sins are covered. Blessed is the man to whom the Lord will not impute sin.*"

Since all humans sin as a result of the "Fall of Man" (The Original Sin), it is impossible for man to become just in our earthly terrestrial bodies. For this reason, we need to be transformed and receive our new sin-free celestial bodies, which believers will receive at the first resurrection (the Rapture).

C. Justification Conditions

1. The atonement of Christ is a condition of justification. The Scriptures below prove that the atonement of Christ is definitely a condition for God to pardon believers:

   (See Rom. 5:6-19, 3:24; Gal. 3:13; Eph. 2:13; Lev. 17:11; Matt. 20:18, 26:28; John 3:14; John 6:51; Acts 20:28; I Cor. 5:7; 1 John 4:9; Heb. 9:12-28).

2. Repentance is another condition of our justification. The sinner must turn from their sins by repenting to God.

> ***Luke 13:3*** *= I tell you, Nay: but, except ye repent, ye shall all likewise perish.*

3. Faith in Christ is also a condition of justification. Faith is a necessary condition of justification. Let the following passages of Scripture convince us: *(see John 1:12, 8:24, 3:16, 11:25-26; Heb. 2:6; Acts 10:43; Mark 14:15-16; Rom. 4:5, 10:4; Acts 16:31)*

4. Sanctification or full consecration to God is a condition of justification. The current dedication of one's heart/life to God and their commitment to God's service is a justification condition *(Psalm 100:2; 1 Pet. 4:10-12)*.

5. Perseverance of faith and consecration to God is an additional condition of justification *(Rev. 2:7; Phil. 1:6)*.

D. *The Calling and Path to Salvation*

God's will is that none would perish. Instead, His desire is that we all will have eternal life *(John 3:16)*. Many are called, but few are chosen *(Matt. 22:14)*. This statement concludes the Wedding Feast Parable. Jesus used this parable to give us some indication of how many actually answer God's call to spend an eternity with Him. Many are not even aware that God is calling them, nor do they care. Lamentably, some are too engaged in worldly affairs, which keep them distracted and prevents them from developing a Godly focus.

For this reason, God commands us not to love the world. Neither should we love the materials which are in this world. Scripture tells us that if someone loves the world, love for the heavenly Father is NOT in him. The world offers sin that includes fleshly lust, the lust of the eyes, and the arrogance or pride of life. These lusts are not of God; instead, they are of this world. This world as we know it will come to an end, and the lust thereof (there will be a new earth, as well as a new heaven), but those that do God's will abide forever *(1 John 2:15-17).*

According to the Wikipedia dictionary, a parable is a succinct, didactic story, in prose or verse that illustrates one or more instructive lessons or principles. A parable is not to be mistaken for a fable. A fable is a succinct fictional literary Genre. A fable is a story, in prose or verse, that features animals, mythical creatures, plants, inanimate objects or forces of nature which are anthropomorphized (given human qualities, such as verbal communication), and that illustrates or leads to an interpretation of a moral lesson (a "moral"). Therefore, a fable differs from a parable in that a parable excludes animals, plants, inanimate objects, and forces of nature as actors that assume speech and other powers of humankind. Additionally, a parable is a type of analogy.[27&28]

In the wedding feast parable, the King sends his servants out to gather the wedding guests to the wedding feast. Some that were invited declined to go because they were too busy filling their schedules with things of the world. Others refused to go because of the hostility that they felt toward the King. So the King asks his servants to go out and invite anyone that they could find. Afterward, many came and filled the wedding hall.

The king sees one man without wedding clothes (referring to those who are not covered by the blood of Christ), and he sends him away. Jesus concludes by saying that many are called or invited to spend eternal life with God, but only those who have believed and received Christ as Lord will be "chosen" or allowed to enter into heaven. Those who want to go to heaven without the covering of Christ for the remission of their sin are not considered to be clothed appropriately to enter God's kingdom and will subsequently spend eternity in the lake of fire.[32]

Many do hear the call of God that comes through revelation. God reveals Himself through two things:

(1) God reveals Himself through the creation.

    (2) And God reveals Himself through the conscience within us.

Few respond with the desire to obey God. Jesus said, "He who has an ear, let him hear . . ." *(Matt. 11:15; Luke 8:8, 14:35).* But, not all of those that hear God's call will respond and receive the Gospel. Many are called into God's kingdom, yet, none will redeem themselves. God will draw man's heart to come to Christ. Otherwise, they fail to accept the Gospel *(John 6:44).*

Eph. 1:4-6 = . . . *he hath chosen us in him before the foundation of the world, that we should be holy and without blame before him in love: Having predestinated us unto the adoption of children by Jesus Christ to himself, according to the good pleasure of his will, To the praise of the glory of his grace, wherein he hath made us accepted in the beloved.*

    Believers were predestined and are adopted as God's children through Jesus. One may ask, "How could this be so if we are free-will agents that have been given an option of accepting Christ as our Redeemer?" Well, let us not forget that this predestination is accomplished by an omniscient and omnipotent God, who is the alpha and omega [the beginning and the ending], and who exists eternally outside of time *(Rev. 22:13).* And because God knew the person that we would choose to become before we even entered our mother's womb, He already knew who would and would not accept His Son, Jesus, as Lord, before we were conceived *(Jer. 1:5).*

Salvation comes as a result of God's will and good pleasure *(John 6:37-39, 44-45).* God predestined those whom He foreknew, and He will tell others to depart from Him because He never knew them *(Matt. 7:23).* God predestines, calls, justifies, and glorifies those that He foreknew, and they take on the image of Jesus Christ *(Rom. 8:30).* Those that have an ear to hear and respond to the call get filled with the Holy Spirit. The Holy Spirit not only fills believers, but He will also comfort us, lead us, guide us, keep us, and assure us of our position with God.

> *Phil. 1:6* = *Being confident of this very thing, that he which hath begun a good work in you will perform it until the day of Jesus Christ:*

We must listen with spiritual ears and respond to God's call. Once one responds to God's call and becomes a child of God, they need to discover and fulfill their God-given purpose. Find your life's divine calling. Some are challenged by this task. One needs to allow the Holy Spirit to direct them.[33]

A **"CALLING"** is God's personal individual invitation to carry out the unique task that He has for us. We need to build a cherished personal relationship with Jesus in order to discover God's specific calling for us individually. Jesus wants to have a special intimate relationship with all believers. Fulfilling God's calling on our lives may be difficult for some, and we won't be successful without God's assistance. With

the guidance and aid of the Holy Spirit, we can accomplish
that which God has appointed us to do. The Holy Spirit will
dwell within us and strengthen us. Greater is He (The Holy
Spirit) that is within us, than He that is in the world. With the
Holy Spirit, we can overcome all obstacles that attempt to
prevent us from fulfilling our God-given purpose in life. [32-33]

Some may be surprised to learn that their job is not
their calling. Their job is an instrument that helps them to
carry out their calling. God equips all of us with unique
spiritual gifts to help us in our calling.

> ***Rom. 12:6-8*** = *Having then gifts differing according to
> the grace that is given to us, whether
> prophecy, let us prophesy according to the
> proportion of faith; Or ministry, let us wait
> on our ministering: or he that teacheth, on
> teaching; Or he that exhorteth, on
> exhortation: he that giveth, let him do it with
> simplicity; he that ruleth, with diligence; he
> that sheweth mercy, with cheerfulness.*

If you have a desire to know, God will make the call on
your life evident to you. Be who God created you to be, and
do not attempt to be someone that you are not. Be led by the
Spirit and give your service to the Lord in a way that pleases
Him. Meditate on God's Word and maintain a strong prayer
life.

> ***Eph. 4:11-15*** = *And he gave some, apostles; and some,
> prophets; and some, evangelists; and some,
> pastors and teachers; For the perfecting of the*

*saints, for the work of the ministry, for the
edifying of the body of Christ: Till we all come
in the unity of the faith, and of the knowledge of
the Son of God, unto a perfect man, unto the
measure of the stature of the fulness of Christ:
That we henceforth be no more children, tossed
to and fro, and carried about with every wind of
doctrine, by the sleight of men, and cunning
craftiness, whereby they lie in wait to deceive;
But speaking the truth in love, may grow up into
him in all things, which is the head, even Christ:*

E. Once You Have Answered God's Call, Is Water Baptism Required for Salvation?

One of the most frequently asked questions concerning salvation is, "Do you need a submerging water baptism to be saved?" According to **Rom. 10:9-10,** one can be saved by simply confessing with the mouth the Lord Jesus and believing in thine heart that God raised him from the dead. The Bible informs us concerning the thief that was crucified with Jesus. He was an example of salvation being given without water baptism. The thief died before having the opportunity to be baptized by water after accepting Jesus as Lord. However, if one is capable of partaking of a submerging water baptism, it should be performed for the following reasons:

1) Water baptism is an important part of Christianity because Jesus was baptized of water. To become a Christian is to be Christ-like. Hence, we should do as

Christ did since He was an example setter for us *(Matt. 3:13-17)*.

2) *Acts 10:47-48* asks if any man could forbid water, that they should not be baptized which have received the Holy Ghost? It further states that it is commanded to be baptized in the name of the Lord *(see also Acts 8:39)*.

3) *John 3:23* indicates that John showed an example of baptism where much water was used (for submerging, not sprinkling). Other examples of baptism can be found in *Acts 8:36* and *Matt. 3:5-6.*

4) Our act of water baptism demonstrates our belief that Jesus died and was raised from the dead (*ref: Rom. 10:9-10* = belief being a requirement for salvation). *Rom. 6:1-8* indicates that we are buried with Jesus by baptism into death and that, like Christ, we shall raise up from the dead and walk in the newness of life. The old creature dies and God creates a new creature in us.

5) *Acts 22:16* is another example that states it is commanded of us to be baptized. It is explained that when we are baptized, our sins are washed away. *Col. 2:4* informs us that water baptism causes our sins to be blotted out and nailed to Calvary's cross *(see also Acts 2:28)*.

6) Our hearts should be true with a full assurance of faith, having our bodies washed with pure water *(Heb. 10:22)*.

7) Another procedure for acquiring salvation is found in *Mark 16:16* = *he that is believeth and is baptized shall*

be saved. Note: This Scripture does NOT denote that salvation will be denied to those that accept the Lord Jesus but neglect water baptism.

8)   *Gal. 3:27* explains that if we are baptized in Christ, then we have put on Christ.

9)   In *Matt. 28:19,* believers are instructed to teach all nations, baptizing them in the name of the Father, the Son, and Holy Spirit. Hence, if for no other reason, we ought to be baptized because we should obey Christ *(ref: 2 Thess. 1:7-8).*

There have been several people who thought that before becoming a Christian, one must rid themselves of all of their sinful practices and live perfectly sin-free. Although it is important for one to consider the lifestyle that they should live as a Christian before accepting Jesus as Lord, it is unreasonable to wait until one is sinless before coming to Jesus for salvation. If we wait until we are faultlessly unflawed before coming to Christ, we would never get saved. We are NOT Jesus and do not have the capability of cleansing ourselves of sin before salvation. If we could redeem ourselves from sin, then there would not have been a need for the coming of Christ. We will never be able to totally abstain from sin in our terrestrial bodies. When we sin, we have an advocate with the Father *(1 John 2:1)*. Have faith that if we will begin our journey with God, the Lord will give us the strength to carry on until the end.[33]

These following are easy steps to take for salvation:

First, one needs to hear the Gospel of Christ (the Good news = God has raised Christ from the dead in order that we may be saved).

Rom. 10:9-10 = That if thou shalt confess with thy mouth the Lord Jesus, and shalt believe in thine heart that God hath raised him from the dead, thou shalt be saved. For with the heart man believeth unto righteousness; and with the mouth confession is made unto salvation.

The Word of God comforts us by informing that God wants all to be saved. Thus, God will send a preacher to deliver the Gospel.

Rom. 10:13-14 = . . . for whosoever shall call upon the name of the lord shall be saved. How then shall they call on him in whom they have not believed? And how shall they believe in him of whom they have not heard? And how shall they hear without a preacher?

After hearing the Word of God (the Gospel – the Good News), one must have faith and believe it to be true.

Secondly, one must confess Jesus as Lord before men with one's mouth. Confessing or accepting Jesus as your Lord and Savior means submission to God's holy will and involves the process of dying to the will of your own flesh. Paul said that he is dying daily, meaning that his fleshly desires were not totally killed instantaneously upon his decision to follow God. This is an indication that becoming a good Christian is a process. In God's sight, we are works in progress. Although our old man dies upon accepting Jesus as Lord, the new creature, which is created in us, is not perfect. We still remain in the contaminated flesh that desires sin. There is a constant battle of flesh against the spirit to overtake one another. By the grace of God and through the Holy Spirit, we must live in the spirit so that the flesh will not provoke us to sin. However, we are saved by grace and not of ourselves *(Eph. 2:8)*. For if we had to be saved by works, we would all be dammed. Because of God's mercy and promise covenant to the seeds of Abraham, He promised to never leave us nor forsake his children. Do not put too much confidence in the flesh because it is the Holy Spirit that dwells within us that gives us the will to abstain from sin.[32&33]

   Thirdly, one must believe in their heart that Jesus was raised from the dead for the remission of their sins in order for us to have a second chance at an eternity with God.

   Fourth, we need to confess/repent of our sins *(Acts 2:38)*.

Acts 2:38 = Then Peter said unto them, repent, and be baptized every one of you in the name of Jesus Christ for the remission of sins, and ye shall receive the gift of the Holy Ghost.

   Fifth, "Submerging Water Baptism" is also an act that believers should perform.

Mark 16:16 = *He that believeth and is baptized shall be saved; but he that believeth not shall be damned.*

Jesus also taught that one should be born of water (the baby's water/amniotic sac in the mother's womb) and of the Spirit (baptism of the Holy Ghost) to inherit God's Kingdom. When someone repents and accepts Jesus as Lord, they are considered to be reborn or born-again.

John 3:5 = *Jesus answered, verily, verily, I say unto thee, except a man be born of water and of the spirit, he cannot enter into the kingdom of god.*

1 Pet. 3:21 = *The like figure whereunto even baptism doth also now save us (not the putting away of the filth of the flesh, but the answer of a good conscience toward god,) by the resurrection of Jesus Christ:*

F. Example of How to Lead Someone to Christ

ALL Christians have all been "**CALLED**" into the ministry of reconciliation *(2 Cor. 5:18)*. Therefore, all Christians are responsible for evangelizing to some degree. There should be an attempt by the Christian Evangelist to meet the needs of the prospect, express the love of God, inference the need for salvation, and to explain the solution using the information above (the steps to salvation).

Believers were also instructed by Jesus to teach the Good News of the Gospel to all nations, baptizing them in the name of the Father, and of the Son, and of the Holy Ghost

(*Matt. 28:19-20*). We must teach others to observe all of the things that our Lord, Jesus, has commanded. This is "The Great Commission" given by Christ for believers.

G. Path to Salvation Synopsis:

Note: One can be saved without water baptism (as was one of the thieves on the cross). However, it is still an important part of Christianity that no one should omit if they have an option.

1. **HEAR THE GOSPEL**
2. **CONFESS JESUS AS LORD**
3. **BELIEVE THAT JESUS WAS RAISED FROM THE DEAD**
4. **CONFESS / REPENT OF ALL SIN**
5. **BAPTISM (SUBMERSION IN WATER AND BAPTISM OF THE HOLY SPIRIT)**

Chapter 8

ELECTION & ETERNAL LIFE

Total depravity is mainly a Calvinist doctrine and is the belief that man's nature is totally corrupt as a result of the original fall of Adam and Eve. Some believe that, as a result of mankind's "total depravity," God chose certain people to be saved prior to their birth. These people that were designated to be saved are called the "elect." They assert that there was nothing different about the chosen elect that caused God to choose them. God is all-powerful, and therefore, has the authority to show grace and mercy to whomever He wants to and can show wrath as He desires. This is considered to be the doctrine of Unconditional Election and implies that God makes decisions without having good reasons for His conclusions.[41]

Calvinist use the following Scriptures (among others) to promote their belief in unconditional election, which is a part of their "T.U.L.I.P." or the "Five Points of Calvinism":

Please read: Mark 13:20; Acts 2:39; Rom. 8:28-30; Eph. 1:1-11; 1 Cor. 1:1; 2 Cor. 4:6; Phil. 1:29; Deut. 7:6-15, Psalms 65:4; 1 Thess. 1:2-4; 2 Thess. 2:13; 2 Tim. 1:9, 2:10, 19, 25; Titus 3:5; Heb. 9:15; James 1:18.

Calvinist generally neglect to explain the basis of God's election. They may even proclaim that God's reasoning for who is selected to become a part of the elect can only truly be understood by God Himself. They consider it to be a mystery that only God knows. They believe that no one can understand how God is able to elect some people and pass over others. They do understand that everything that God decides is righteous and that God does NOT make mistakes.[41]

Some do not believe in unconditional election because they consider it to be unfair for God to select/elect some who do not differ from others and save the elect while damning the rest. They think that this would be an unjust action by God that would defy God's sovereign character. If all of humanity were to receive what is fair, then all would be burned in the lake of fire. God does not owe mankind any favors. He does not have to bless us with His grace and mercy. If He does, it's because of His unconditional love for humans. God shows mercy by sparing the elect from an eternal damnation.[41]

Since the fall of man in the Garden of Eden, all men are born with the inability to resist all sin. We have all sinned in one way or another. God has infinite wisdom and knowledge.

Unlike man, He is omniscient, so He knew during the election process who would accept Jesus as their Lord and desire Him to become their Savior. Calvinist's don't believe that God's foreknowledge had anything to do with His election decisions. They insinuate that God ignored His foreknowledge of man's acceptance of Jesus when He made the decision during the election process for that individual. If so, why would Jesus need to die on Mount Calvary's cross? Unconditional election suggests that the death of Jesus was unnecessary and in vain.[41]

Calvinist's think that after God elected certain sinners to be saved, He predestined them for salvation. When one elects something or someone, they choose them. To predestine something or someone is to decide the outcome prior to the event. The difference between election and predestination is the variance between choice and power. Election and predestination are two separate but inseparable actions. When God elects, He predestines, and when He declares that something will happen, it happens. Man's salvation is dependent on our repentance and acceptance of Jesus as Lord.[41]

Additionally, Calvinist's believe that sinners are chosen to be saved but are not saved yet. According to them, an elect person remains ungodly until God draws them to the Son through regeneration. The choice of the person's salvation is decided in eternity past. This would make God somewhat of a puppet master and would mean that man does not have free-will.

On the contrary, man does have free-will that is given by God. Mankind has utilized free-will since the beginning of time. This utilization of free-will is what caused the first sin of Adam and Eve in the midst of the garden where they were forbidden to eat of the tree of good and evil *(Gen.)*. Satan also has free-will, which caused him to fall like lightning from heaven because he decided that he would rather be worshipped as a god than to worship Jehovah God *(Luke 10:18)*.[41]

We are saved by grace through faith, which comes from hearing the Gospel, and hearing by the Word of God *(Eph. 2:8-9; Rom. 10:17)*. Anyone who believes the Gospel shall be saved *(Rom. 1:16-17)*. The Gospel is preached, Man receives the Good News, and as a result, man is saved *(Matt. 28:19-20)*. God also commissioned man to spread His Word.[41]

Calvinists say that God's foreknowledge is His ability to read or predict the future. They assume that humans don't have the ability to have faith in Jesus without God causing their faith. Conversely, faith is a gift from God, and God does not force the gift on anyone *(Eph. 2:8)*. God lets people choose which god(s) or God that they want to serve. The Calvinist's view or interpretation of unconditional election has continued to spread throughout other denominations since John Calvin's era and has misled masses.[41]

The Biblical doctrine of election is not a matter of man being chosen for salvation so that they can be saved without repentance, faith, and sanctification. People are not chosen to salvation without being regenerated and without faithfulness to God. The Bible explains to us that these are conditions of salvation. Election does not negate the conditions of salvation. Keep in mind that salvation is not granted to one based on their own good works, and yet, faith without works is dead *(James 2:20)*.[41]

> *2 Tim. 1:9 =* *Who hath saved us, and called us with a holy calling, not according to our works, but according to his own purpose and grace, which was given us in Christ Jesus before the world began."*

God did not elect some to salvation because of their goodness but for the reason of their foreseen repentance, faith, perseverance, and submission to our Redeemer, Jesus. The Biblical doctrine of election does NOT (as the Calvinists believe) indicate, that God elected some to salvation NOT knowing whether or not those who He elected will comply with His conditions. He knew all of us before our birth *(Jer. 1:5)*. God knew who would submit to His authority before our lives began at childbirth. It is critical to understand that the elect were chosen for salvation based on God's foreknowledge of man's free-will decisions. God knew beforehand that He could secure the repentance, faith, and final perseverance of the elect.[41]

Humans were called by God to eternal salvation through the sanctification by faith in Christ. They are chosen to salvation by their sanctification. Salvation is the result of one's sanctification. We must realize that sanctification is a means for salvation and that the sanctification process does not start until one repents, submits to God's authority, and accepts Jesus as Lord and Savior. There is no other way to the Father but through His Son, Jesus. This means that there is no other way to be saved except through the redeeming blood of Christ. The end and the means of sanctification are elected, appointed, and chosen.[41]

> *Matt.* **20:16** = *So the last shall be first, and the first last, for many be called, but few chosen.*

> *Matt.* **24:22** = *And except those days should be shortened, there should no flesh be saved; but for the elect's sake those days shall be shortened.*

> *John* **13:18** = *I speak not of you all; I know whom I have chosen . . .*

> *John* **15:16-19** = *Ye have not chosen me, but I have chosen you, and ordained you, that ye should go and bring forth fruit, and that your fruit should remain; that whatsoever ye shall ask of the*

Father in my name, he may give it you . . . If ye were of the world, the world would love his own; but because ye are not of the world, but I have chosen you out of the world, therefore the world hateth you.

Rom. 8:28-29 = *And we know that all things work together for good to them that love God, to them who are the called according to his purpose. For whom he did foreknow, he also did predestinate to be conformed to the image of his Son, that he might be the first-born among many brethren.*

Rom. 9:10-15 = *And not only this, but when Rebecca had conceived by one, even by our father Isaac; For the children being not yet born, neither having done any good or evil, that the purpose of God according to election might stand, not of works, but of him that calleth.) It was said unto her, the elder shall serve the younger. As it is written, Jacob have I loved, but Esau have I hated. What shall we say then? Is there unrighteousness with God? God forbid. For he saith to Moses, I will have mercy on whom I will have mercy, and I will have compassion on whom I will have compassion.*

Rom. 11:5, 7 = *Even so then at this present time also there is a remnant according to the election of grace . . . What then? Israel hath not obtained that which he seeketh for, but the election hath obtained it, and the rest were blinded.*

Eph. 1:4, 11 = *According as he hath chosen us in him before the foundation of the world, that we should be holy and without blame before him in*

*love . . . In whom also we have obtained an
inheritance, being predestinated according to
the purpose of him who worketh all things after
the counsel of his own will.*

1 Thess. 1:4 = *Knowing, brethren beloved, your
election of God.*

1 Thess. 5:9 = *For God hath not appointed us to wrath,
but to obtain salvation by our Lord Jesus Christ.*

2 Thess. 2:13 = *But we are bound to give thanks always
to God for you, brethren beloved of the Lord,
because God hath from the beginning chosen
you to salvation through sanctification of the
Spirit, and belief of the truth.*

1 Pet. 1:2 = *Elect according to the foreknowledge of
God the Father, through sanctification of the
Spirit, unto obedience and sprinkling of the
blood of Jesus Christ.*

Rev. 17:8 = *the beast that thou sawest was, and is not;
and shall ascend out of the bottomless pit, and
go into perdition: and they that dwell on the
earth shall wonder, (whose names were not
written in the book of life from the foundation of
the world,) when they behold the beast that was,
and is not, and yet is."*

If God knows who will be saved now, he must have
always known it. If not, this would mean that He obtained
new knowledge, which contradicts His omniscient character.

Yes, God always knew who would be saved, and He did not choose the elect without reason. God does not haphazardly do anything. Everything that God does is with purpose. Those that God will ever save were from eternity past, chosen to salvation by Him, and were saved by means of sanctification. This was eternally designed and intended by God. We can't deny the doctrine of election; otherwise, we deny God's attributes. Moreover, we must not misinterpret the meaning of election by removing Jesus from the subject.[41]

God foreknew everything concerning the non-elect, and He had specific plans concerning their final destiny (damnation). Know that God is infinitely compassionate and judicious. For this reason, we can be assured that election is purposed for good cause. God can NOT be evaluated based on our interpretation of what is just.

Election does NOT mean that God is partial or prejudice against any. God has necessary and sufficient motives for electing some and rejecting others. He did not choose the elect arbitrarily. Some assume that God did not have good reasons for His elect selection. Again, they ignore God's omniscience. Since God knows all and has always known all, He was able to utilize the best means of election selection.[41]

CAN THE ELECT BE DECEIVED into following a false prophet or god? Consider:

> *Matt. 24:24* = *For there shall arise false Christ's, and false prophets, and shall show great signs and wonders; in so much that if it were possible, they shall deceive the very elect.*

This Scripture is telling us that the VERY ELECT CAN <u>NOT</u> BE DECEIVED. God knew beforehand who would and would not be deceived into following false gods and rejecting Christ. His foreknowledge allows Him to select the elect. Those that reject Christ are considered to be anti-Christ. Those who worship Satan shall NOT be saved from eternal damnation. Once a person truly accepts membership into this VERY ELECT group, the knowledge of our true and holy God shall not be forgotten. God blesses His children not only with the gift of salvation, but He offers believers the spiritual gift of discernment, which can be used to distinguish good versus evil *(1 Cor. 12, 14)*.[41]

The spiritual gift of discernment gives the ability to detect or perceive whether people, events, or beliefs are of God or Satan. Believers with the gift of discernment know that Satan and his demons disguise themselves as wolves in sheep's clothing *(1 Cor. 11:14-15)*. Be aware of the fact that Satan will even cause counterfeit miracles in an attempt to be like the "Most-High God," Jehovah *(Exod. 7:11-22, 8:7; Matt. 7:21-23; 2 Tim. 3:8)*. He does this with the purpose of deceiving people so that they will turn from God and worship him *(2 Thess. 2:9).* He empowers and enables FALSE teachers, prophets, apostles, and doctrines *(1 Tim. 1:3, 6:3; 2 Pet. 2:1; Matt. 7:15; 2 Cor. 11:13).*[41]

Some that are misled by false teachings will leave their deceptive misleading groups, which influenced their thoughts, beliefs, and/or actions. Even though they may have overcome the deception, they were not a part of the VERY ELECT from the beginning. In *Matt. 24:24*, there is a warning to God's very elect about the coming end-time Satanic delusions. These delusions are evil trickery of the devil, and the deceit is amplified near the end of the church age. Christ gave this same caution in *Matt. 24:5-11*.

Each warning signifies Satan's intentional intensification to destroy God's children. The deception becomes greater and greater as Satan's time of reigning on earth is running out. Deceivers will come in the end-times attempting to cause the elect to turn from God. These lying frauds will give an appearance of Godliness and pretend to speak the truth. Paul's warns us about these misleaders when he spoke to the Corinthians. The genuine elect will withstand their guile and shall NOT be deceived.[41]

2 Cor. 11:13-15= For such are false apostles, deceitful workers, transforming themselves into the apostles of Christ. And no marvel; for Satan himself is transformed into an angel of light. Therefore it is no great thing if his ministers also be transformed as the ministers of righteousness; whose end shall be according to their works.

Thanks to these Biblical forewarnings, we should not be faced with these issues unexpectedly. Satan is evil, and he can cunningly appear as an angel of light. His works will be considered by many to be signs and wonders. God allows Satan's deceit as a part of the process of the building of His eternal kingdom. It is out of love that the elect must obey the Laws that are given by God. In order to detect Satan's lies, we should know and understand God's truth. God's Word provides truth that we need to understand Him and helps us to be prepared for what is coming at the end of this age.[41]

1 Pet. 5:8-10 tells us to be sober and vigilant (watchful and alert) because the adversary or devil walks about like a roaring lion, seeking whom he may devour. We must resist Satan's temptations, and maintain our faith in our Father, Jehovah God *(James 4:7)*. Our love of the truth and God's Holy Spirit that dwells within us keeps us from being deceived by Satan's deviousness.

God's Biblical warnings imply that there is a possibility that man has the potential to fail.[41]

1 Cor. 10:12 = *Wherefore let him that thinketh he standeth take heed lest he fall.*

2 Tim. 2:14-18 = *Of these things put them in remembrance, charging them before the Lord that they strive not about words to no profit, but to the subverting of the hearers. Study to shew thyself approved unto God, a workman that needeth not to be ashamed, rightly dividing the word of truth. But shun profane and vain babblings: for they will increase unto more ungodliness. And their word will eat as doth a canker: of whom is Hymenaeus and Philetus; Who concerning the truth have erred, saying that the resurrection is past already; and OVERTHROW THE FAITH OF SOME.*

We learn from Scripture that some people will be lost.

2 Pet. 3:15-18 = *And account that the longsuffering of our Lord is salvation; even as our beloved brother Paul also according to the wisdom given unto him hath written unto you; As also in all his epistles, speaking in them of these things; in which are some things hard to be understood, which they that are unlearned and unstable wrest, as they do also the other scriptures, unto their own destruction. Ye therefore, beloved, seeing ye know these things before, beware lest ye also, being led away with the error of the wicked, fall from your own stedfastness. But grow in grace, and in the knowledge of our Lord and Saviour Jesus Christ. To him be glory both now and for ever. Amen.*

Some of the New Testament was written to prevent mankind from failing. However, although believers are blessed by the offer of the spiritual gift of discernment, this does not mean that it is impossible for believers to be tempted to sin. If we detect deception, it is by the power of the Holy Spirit. Knowing that we are vulnerable can keep us vigilant. Our alertness and watchfulness are essential because Satan is equipped with great wiles. Remember, he would deceive the elect "IF" it were possible. Notice the word "IF" in the "if it were possible" statement.

According to Webster's Dictionary, one of the definitions of the word "IF" means "on the assumption that." By this definition, deception "IS" possible "IF" we carelessly make decisions without being led by the Holy Spirit. We must try the spirit by the Spirit or Holy Ghost. When false prophets contradict the Holy Scripture, we need to be on our guard. We should not put our trust in them; rather, we must trust in God and His Word.

An assumption is a postulation, which is a mere guess. "IF" it were possible, gives an indication that it is not possible; however, that Scripture does NOT specifically and definitely state that it is NOT possible for the elect to be deceived (because of the use of the word "IF"). Furthermore, the use of the word "IF" hints that it is possible for the elect to be deceived, yet, makes some think that it is not likely probable.[41]   Let's not forget that God foreknew the outcome of Satan's deceit when selecting the elect.

Did Christ create a special category of the elect that were mentioned in *Matt. 24:24*? Did he create the VERY ELECT as a group that is set apart from the regular ELECT? The word for "elect" is number 1,588 in Strong's. It is used twenty-three times in the New Testament. The only place that the word elect (#1,588) is modified by the word "very" (#2,532) is in *Matt. 24:24* in the King James translation. The companion Scripture of *Mark 13:22* uses the same combination of words, but the word "very" (#2,532) is translated "even" here.

It is not certain, but many believe that if Christ was creating a new category for the elect, we would be able to find it in other Passages. But it is not found anywhere else except in *Matt. 24:24*. The Concise Oxford Dictionary defines "very" as real, true, and genuine. Webster's says that the word "very" is used to emphasize that you are talking about one specific thing or part, and not another. The word "very" emphasizes identity or significance and brings the noun into special prominence. "Very" can also mean "not having anything added or extra." Therefore, many believe that *Matt. 24:24* refers to the same group of the elect that is mentioned in other Scriptures.[41]

To believe that humans cannot be deceived suggests that man is infallible. God's gift of discernment helps, and the guidance of the Holy Spirit aids. But humans are not all knowing and can be deceived like Eve was in the Garden of Eden. It is not God's will for man to be confused. He is not the author of confusion *(1 Cor. 14:33)*. Nevertheless, Christ did not establish an infallible group of the elect. The only time that man is incapable of being deceived and tempted to sin is after death. While a person lives, it is the job of the Holy Spirit to keep believers faithful to God until the end. Therefore, let him who thinks he stands, take heed, lest he falls *(1 Cor. 10:12)*.[41]

Believers or the chosen elect, are typically known by their character. Their submission to God affects their behavior and is evidence of their election. When we repent and confess that Jesus is our Lord, we are filled with God's Holy Spirit. By submitting to God, one can expect integrity betterment.

After the infilling of the Holy Spirit, the person that is filled may see evidence of it by receiving the spiritual gift of speaking in tongues. This is one of the nine gifts of the Spirit, and there are various types of speaking in tongues. These include two public and two private ways of speaking in tongues.

A. *Public Types of Speaking in Tongues:*

(1) – Speaking in tongues can be a sign for unbelievers.

> ***1 Cor. 14:22*** = *Wherefore tongues are for a sign, not to them that believe, but to them that believe not: but prophesying serveth not for them that believe not, but for them which believe.*

The Holy Spirit transcends one's intellect, and they may begin praying, speaking, preaching, prophesying, or teaching in a language that is known to other people, but it is an earthly language that they have never learned. This occurs in ***Acts 2***. The disciples had come together in the upper room during Pentecost when the Holy Ghost filled them. As a result, they commenced speaking in other tongues, as the Holy Spirit caused them to utter. At that time, Jews that came from every nation resided in Jerusalem. A multitude of them came together and were confused by the realization of every man hearing the disciples speaking in their own languages. They understood this event to be a great work of God.

(2) – Speaking in tongues with an interpretation in public can edify the church.

> ***1 Cor. 14:5*** *= I would that ye all spake with tongues, but rather that ye prophesied: for greater is he that prophesieth than he that speaketh with tongues, except he interpret, that the church may receive edifying.*

This form of speaking in tongues occurs in an assembly where the Holy Spirit comes upon a person and they begin to speak in a heavenly language with an interpretation of what was said *(1 Cor. 12, 14).* God has certain rules that apply when speaking in tongues. For example, ***1 Cor. 14:27-28*** informs us that if anyone speaks in an **unknown tongue, let it be by two, or at the most by three, and let one interpret. But if there is no interpreter, let him keep silence in the church**; and let him speak to himself, and to God.

B. *Private Types of Speaking in Tongues:*

(1) – Some may speak with a groaning during intercessory prayer, petitions, or entreaties in concern for others.

> ***Rom. 8:26-27*** *= Likewise the Spirit also helpeth our infirmities: for we know not what we should pray for as we ought: but the Spirit itself maketh intercession for us with groanings which cannot be uttered. And he that searcheth the hearts knoweth what is the mind*

of the Spirit, because he maketh intercession for the saints according to the will of God.

This groaning intercession is done for someone else when one does not know what the prayer needs to accomplish. The groaning is an unutterable gushing from the heart *(see also: Acts 7:34).* The Holy Spirit, our "Paraclete" or Helper, makes intercession for the saints to accomplish the necessary tasks. Some believers do not consider groaning to be a form of speaking in tongues, because tongues mean languages, and they say that groans are not a language. Contrarily, according to Webster's Dictionary, a language can be a system of signs that people use to express thoughts or feelings. Because of this definition, many considered intercessory groaning to be a language or tongue.

(2) Believers may also speak in tongues during personal prayer, which results in personal edification.

> *1 Cor. 14:4 = He that speaketh in an unknown tongue edifieth himself; but he that prophesieth edifieth the church.*

Paul explains why we should pray in the Spirit in an unknown heavenly tongue, as well as praying in an earthly known language that we are familiar with. The unknown tongue is understood by God, yet demonic forces can NOT interpret. Hence, evil spirits won't attempt to interfere with your prayer getting answered or effect the outcome of it because they will not know what was prayed.

> ***1 Cor. 14:14-15*** = *For if I pray in an unknown tongue, my spirit prayeth, but my understanding is unfruitful. What is it then? I will pray with the spirit, and I will pray with the understanding also: I will sing with the spirit, and I will sing with the understanding also.*

> ***Jude 1:20*** = *But ye, beloved, building up yourselves on your most holy faith, praying in the Holy Ghost,*

All of mankind has the option of submitting to God. They can either accept or reject God's gift of salvation. The elect are saved by their faith, and the non-elect will receive their penalty of sin (the second death) because of their rejection of Jesus.[41]

The elect were chosen for eternal life with God because God foresaw that they utilized their free-will by repenting, submitting to Jesus, and accepting God's Word. Some misinterpret the doctrine of election and deduce unjustifiable inferences from it. They assume that the doctrine of election means that the elect will be saved regardless of their choices or actions. They think that salvation is not possible for the non-elect, despite their conduct or the choices that they make. If their interpretation regarding the elect and salvation held true, sin would be encouraged and go unpunished. Knowing that their salvation was secure, why would the elect need or want to experience the sanctification process? Why would they need to obey God? Why would they need to live holy? Satan has misled them into believing that they may sin as much as they desire and still receive God's best.[41]

Election does not secure the salvation of the elect regardless of the person's disposition, choices, character, or actions. Nor does election cause people to be damned. No one can do whatever they want without penalties for disobedience to God's will just because they are predestined to be elect. The sinner's damnation is definitely a result of their own decision. Both the elect and the non-elect should both be grateful for God allowing man to utilize our gift of free-will. Surely, the elect should be thankful for their predestinated salvation. The names of the elect are written in the Lamb's Book of Life. They are chosen by God to be heirs of eternal salvation, to be adopted into His family, to be joint-heirs with Christ Jesus, and to spend all eternity with God, the Father. It is a marvelous blessing to receive a new celestial body or a heavenly body that is sinless. Imagine never being tempted to sin again. This alone is praiseworthy.[41]

The non-elect should also be thankful. They should be grateful for God giving them an opportunity to accept His gift of salvation, even if they do not decide to accept it. We all should appreciate God for offering us a choice. We should be grateful to God for saving any of our family members or friends. We should all value the choice of accepting the gift of salvation because none of us deserve it. All have sinned in some manner, so, we do not deserve to be redeemed by Christ and are unworthy of God's gift. Since the penalty of sin is death, if God damned us all, He would still be just. Therefore, when any non-believer repents and accepts Jesus as Lord, we should all celebrate their victory over the second death and eternal damnation.[41]

Dejectedly, many hear the Good News and ignore it, so they die in their sins. Others are converted to Christianity after hearing the Gospel of Christ. Generally, the elect possess more of God's character than the non-elect. Even the unbelievers may feel some sort of conviction for their sins; yet, they have subjected themselves to evil deceitful lies which cause them to love the world and oppose God. This is why their eternal future will exist in the lake of fire with Satan, whom they served/followed on earth. They give in to sin by their own free-will desires.[41]

Some wonder why God uses the method that He does for determining who will be considered the non-elect. We must know that these decisions must be made according to God's will and not our own *(Matt. 26:39)*. God desires that man be without excuse. Hence, do not attempt to justify evil doings. God will allow people to demonstrate their own actions, their willingness to submit to Him, or their refusal to succumb to His will. When a person is judged by God, one's rejection of the salvation offer will enhance their guilt of sin. God foreknows who will reject His gift of salvation; however, He still offers it to both the elect and the non-elect. This shows God's love for all of humanity and His willingness/desire to save us all. Still, some refuse God's grace.[41]

God has placed the responsibility of choosing life or death (blessing or cursing) upon every individual *(Deut. 30:19)*. Those that have warm blood flowing through their veins still have the option of choosing salvation rather than damnation. On the other hand, we all also have the right and ability to reject Jesus and inherit the hellfire in eternal torment. This lake of eternal fire offers a home of suffering where there will be no rest. Let him that hears the Good News come *(Rev. 22:17)*. Whosoever will, let them come to Christ? Jesus stands at the door and knocks; it is our responsibility to answer the door.[41]

God did not choose the elect when the elect are converted into believers. God has known all things perfectly from eternity past. God is unchangeable and has always had all the knowledge of all past, present, and future events *(Mal.*

3:6). He chose the elect from eternity past in respect to all

events. The choice of election is an eternal choice.[41]

> ***Eph. 1:4*** = *According as he hath chosen us in him*
> *before the foundation of the world, that we*
> *should be holy and without blame before him in*
> *love.*

> ***Eph. 2:10*** = *For we are his workmanship, created in*
> *Christ Jesus unto good works, which God hath*
> *before ordained that we should walk in them.*

> ***2 Tim. 1:9*** = *Who hath saved us, and called us with a*
> *holy calling; not according to our works, but*
> *according to his own purpose and grace, which was*
> *given us in Christ Jesus before the world began.*

> ***Rev. 17:8*** = *The beast that thou sawest was, and is not,*
> *and shall ascend out of the bottomless pit, and go*
> *into perdition: and they that dwell on the earth shall*
> *wonder, (whose names were not written in the book*
> *of life from the foundation of the world,) when they*
> *behold the beast that was, and is not, and yet is.*

God's foreknowledge preceded election. Prior to the

believer's conversion, God knew whom he could save.

Election is not the reason for the salvation of the chosen ones.

Nor are unbelievers damned due to their non-election. Since

the God that we serve is holy, just, and sovereign, trust that

His election is just. We must obtain our own election through

faith in Jesus. And God foreknew our faith potential.[41]

Chapter 9

ARE ANY PREDESTINED?

Predestination is God's way of ordaining salvation for mankind before they were even aware that they need it. It is the doctrine that God has established in advance concerning what is going to happen in the future regarding the eternal lives of humans. God knew at the beginning of time whose names would be found in the Lamb's Book of Life. The English word "predestination" is not found in the KJV Bible. We can find the Greek verb for predestinate occurring four times in **Rom. 8:29-30** and **Eph. 1:5-11**. The word means to determine or ordain beforehand. The word *predestinate* (*proorizo*) is closely related to three other more frequently used Biblical words.[27&35]

1. TO "DETERMINE"
2. TO "ELECT"
3. TO "FOREKNOW"

Each of these represents various Greek and Hebrew words. The main Scriptures that are related to predestination include *Rom. 8, Eph. 1,* and *1 Pet. 1*. The Book of Acts refers to God's purpose for determining who is to be considered as a part of the elect. We learn that Jesus is God's predetermined Savior *(Acts 2:23, 11:29, 17:26, 2:23,* and *10:41-42)*. We learn of Paul's famous battle of the flesh and of the Spirit in *Rom. 7-8*. *Rom. 7* explains how the Law affects lives. The Law provides us with commands regarding what to do and what not to do. However, the Law does NOT instruct us on how to keep the commands of the Law. Sin causes humans to constantly struggle. Therefore, if there were specific instructions that informed us on how to keep the commandments, we would still fail in keeping them. God's Holy Spirit enables us to do God's will.[24]

Rom. 8 discusses the life in the Spirit, salvation, and the spiritual struggle, etc. Predestination is referenced in *Rom. 29-30*. Some consider these Scriptures to be Paul's way of explaining the struggle with human willfulness, divine purpose, and guidance. Paul understood that God has good intentions for mankind, and He helps us with our struggles. Believers must conform to the image of Christ, our Redeemer. God's Holy Spirit that dwells within believers helps us to be more like Jesus during our conformation process.[24]

Some believe that God made all decisions and planned things beforehand without any regard for human response. This suggests that God would take good people, harden their hearts, and turn them into someone evil. The truth is that God is no respecter of persons, and He does not violate man's God-given free-will.[35]

In *Eph. 1,* we find expressions of God's purpose. People hear the message of the Gospel, believe it, receive the Holy Spirit, and begin to live under submission to Jesus as their Lord. God allowed Jesus to be sacrificed as a part of His redemptive plan for eternal salvation. Through Jesus, we can commune with and develop relations with God, the Father, and are reconciled back to Him. By the omniscient power of God's Holy Spirit, as we believe in Christ with faith, we are predestined and elected. God knows the hearts of men. Prior to our births, God knew who would have faith, believe, and accept His Son as Lord. He knew who would and who would not receive Christ when He selected the predestined elect or chosen people. Hypothetically, if you had foreknowledge that the NFL Denver Broncos would lose to the Seattle Seahawks because you were all-knowing, would that mean that you intentionally caused the Broncos to lose? Of course not; just because you knew beforehand that something was going to happen, does NOT mean that you caused that event to occur.

Likewise, God having the power to make an event occur does not mean that He unquestionably caused it to happen.[35]

God wills that people would utilize their free-will and gladly serve Him. ***Rom. 7*** and the Book of ***Eph.*** indicate that we can exercise our God-given free-will and refuse to serve and believe in God. God will allow us to be disobedient. Predestination never eliminates human will.[35]

In ***1 Peter 1:2,*** we find the prelude or greeting of the author to the readers in the name of the foreknowing Father, the sanctifying Holy Spirit, and the sacrificing Son. In this Scripture, we see exhortations to Christian living, as well as Jesus dying according to God's plan ***(Luke 22:22; Acts 2:23).*** Jesus willingly participated in God's redeeming plan that involved Him brutally dying for the reconciliation of all mankind. We learn that the twelve apostles were hand chosen by God ***(Acts 10:41).*** It is only appropriate for God to determine the parameters of mankind ***(Acts 17:26).*** We should shadow the image of Christ in our efforts to do God's will according to His plan and purposes.[35]

Paul said that Judaism is God's preparation for the fullness of Christ. One of the primary assignments for believers is to deliver the Good News or the Gospel of Christ to all of the earth ***(Mark 16:15).*** The purpose of predestination is to conform mankind into goodness through the power of the Holy Spirit and by bearing witness to the Lord Jesus. Satan discovered that Judas was willing to betray Jesus, so he persuaded Judas to transgress against God *(John 13:27).* We all experience Satan's temptation to sin against God. We must resist the Devil so that he will flee *(James 4:7).* Judas neglected to resist Satan's temptation as a result of his own free-will choice and greed.[35]

Some wonder, if God is sovereign, how could He give humans a free-will to sin against Him? Indeed, God is sovereign. For this reason, God allows man to make free-will decisions and decide whether or not they desire to spend an eternity with our Holy Lord.

If not, they reject Christ, which results in their spending an eternity in the lake of fire with their false lord, Satan. Humans were created to serve. It is in our nature. In one's lack of service to God, they serve Satan and aid in accomplishing his wicked objectives.[35]

God offers the grace of salvation to believers and withholds it from unbelievers. God does show grace on whomever He pleases and shows His wrath on others as He pleases *(Rom. 9:15).* God typically shows believers more grace than He shows unbelievers. If God decreed that some are to be saved, when He decreed this, He knew that they would, in time, submit to His authority with faith.

Additionally, He has predestined others to damnation, knowing at the time in which He predestined this, that they would remain unbelievers that will refuse Christ and deny His Lordship. Jesus must first be our Lord before He will become our Savior. When Jesus is our Lord, we acknowledge Him to be a higher ranking official than ourselves. He is someone whom we understand to be more powerful than ourselves, and we acknowledge His authority over us. We submit to Him as our master and ruler.

The church is considered to be the Body of Christ, and Jesus is the Head of our church. Predestination is an assurance of God's redemptive love for the Body of Christ.[35]

A. *Jew, Israelite, Judaism, Rabbinic Judaism, Orthodox/Hasidic Judaism, Messianic Judaism, Conservative Judaism, Reconstructionist Judaism, and Reformed Judaism*

There are many sorts of Judaism. Understanding certain terms help us comprehend God's relationship with Israel and the salvation of His chosen people. An **"Israelite"** is a descendant of the Hebrew patriarch Jacob, who is a native or inhabitant of the ancient northern kingdom of Israel. A **"Jew"** is a member of the people and cultural community whose traditional religion is Judaism and who trace their origins through the ancient Hebrew people of Israel to Abraham. I will explain some of the major types of Judaism.[2&3]

"Judaism" is the religion of the Jewish people. It is an ancient, monotheistic, Abrahamic religion with the Torah as its foundational text. It encompasses the religion, philosophy, and culture of the Jewish people. Judaism is considered by religious Jews to be the expression of the covenant that God established with the Children of Israel. Judaism encompasses a wide amount of texts, practices, theological positions, and forms of organization. Judaism is the tenth largest religion in the world.[1&2]

"Rabbinic Judaism" believe that God revealed his laws and commandments to Moses on Mount Sinai in the form of both the Written and Oral Torah.[1&2]

"Orthodox / Hasidic Judaism" is a major branch within Judaism that teaches strict adherence to the rabbinical interpretation of Jewish law and its traditional observances. An **"Orthodox Jew"** is a person who adheres faithfully to the principles and practices of traditional Judaism as evidenced chiefly by a devotion to and study of the Torah, daily synagogue attendance if possible, and strict observance of the Sabbath, religious festivals, holy days, and the dietary laws. Those of the Orthodox affiliation, do not consider Jesus to be the Jewish Messiah.[1&2]

"Messianic Judaism" is a movement of Jews who believe that Jesus (called by them with his Hebrew name "Yeshua") is the Jewish Messiah. They practice this belief in a Jewish way (observing the regulations of the Torah, etc.). They are called Messianic Jews.[1&2]

"Conservative Judaism" (also known as **Masorti Judaism** outside of North America) is a major Jewish denomination, which views Jewish Law, or Halakha, as both binding and subject to historical development. The Conservative rabbis use modern historical research, rather than only traditional methods and sources, and lends great weight to its constituency when determining its stance on matters of Law.[1&2]

"Reconstructionist Judaism" is a modern Jewish movement that views Judaism as a progressively evolving civilization and is based on the conceptions developed by Mordecai Kaplan (1881–1983). The movement originally was semi-organized within Conservative Judaism and developed from the late 1920s to 1940s before it was successful in 1955 and a rabbinical college was established in 1967. [1]   There is substantial theological diversity within the movement. The Jewish Law is not considered binding and is treated as a valuable cultural remnant that should be upheld. The movement also has positive views on modernism and has an approach to Jewish custom which aims toward communal

decision-making through the education and distillation of values from traditional Jewish sources.[1&2]

"Reformed Judaism" (also known as **"Liberal Judaism"** or **"Progressive Judaism"**) is a major Jewish denomination that emphasizes the evolving nature of the faith, the superiority of its ethical aspects to the ceremonial ones, and a belief in a continuous revelation not centered on the theophany at Mount Sinai. A liberal strand of Judaism, it is characterized by a lesser stress on ritual and personal observance, regarding Jewish Law as non-binding and the individual Jew as autonomous, and openness to external influences and progressive values. The origins of Reform Judaism lay in nineteenth-century Germany, where its early principles were formulated by Rabbi Abraham Geiger and his associates. Since the 1970s, the movement adopted a policy of inclusiveness and acceptance, inviting as many as possible to partake in its communities rather than strict theoretical clarity. Its greatest center today is in North America.[1&2]

The various regional branches sharing these beliefs, including the American Union for Reform Judaism (URJ), the Movement for Reform Judaism (MRJ) and Liberal Judaism in Britain, and the Israel Movement for Reform and Progressive Judaism, are all united within the international World Union for Progressive Judaism.[1&2]

B. Evaluation of Rom. 11:26 - "All Israel Shall Be Saved"

In *Rom. 11:26*, Paul declares that ". . . **ALL ISRAEL SHALL BE SAVED** . . ." This is a powerful, yet controversial statement. This Scripture has caused many questions to arise. Much of the debate is over who is included in "ALL ISRAEL." Consider the following more popular opinions on how to interpret what is meant by "ALL ISRAEL" in this Scripture:

1. "All Israel" is believed by some to mean **every Jewish person that ever lived.** They think that every Jew is automatically considered to be a part of the elect and predestined for salvation. This view claims that any Jew who considered himself as a Jew according to the Law of Moses and the traditions of the Rabbis is saved. This view is not accepted by many because Jesus said, without exemptions, *"except ye repent, ye shall ALL likewise perish" - (Luke 13:3)*. Another reason that this view is not accepted is that in *Rom. 3,* Jesus asks, who is my mother or brothers? Jesus said, that *whosoever shall do the will of God, the same is my brother, and my sister, and mother (Mark 3:31-35)*. Jesus confirms that all who do God's will are His family. Hence, this indicates that more than a bloodline is required for salvation. In addition, Esaias said that

although the number of the children of Israel may be as sea sand, only a remnant shall be saved *(Rom. 9:27).* A remnant is a part of something and not the entire bunch.

2. Secondly, "All Israel" is believed by some to mean **a chosen remnant of elect Jews.** With this view, Jewish believers of ethnic Israel that have been saved, are thought to be what is meant by "All Israel." This idea specifies that God only hardened the hearts of a partial remnant of the Jews for the purpose of redemption. One may have problems believing this view because God is NOT a respecter of persons *(Rom. 2:11; Acts 10:34).* Furthermore, God warns us in *Rom. 2:12* (without excluding Israel)*,* that as many as have sinned without law shall perish without law, and as many as have sinned in the law shall be judged by the law. Also, Jesus explained that He is the way, the truth, and the life: NO MAN can come to the Father, but by Him *(John 14:6; Acts 4:12).* This Scripture appears to include those that are of Israel.

> ***John 3:36*** = *He that believeth on the Son hath everlasting life: and he that believeth not the Son shall not see life; but the wrath of God abideth on him.*

> *1 John 2:22-23* = *Who is a liar but he that denieth that Jesus is the Christ? He is antichrist, that denieth the Father and the Son. Whosoever denieth the Son, the same hath not the Father: (but) he that acknowledgeth the Son hath the Father also.*

3. Thirdly, "All Israel" is believed by some to mean **ethnic Israel,** and it is believed that they will receive salvation at the **end of days** after the elect gentiles have been renewed *(Rom. 11:25)*. This interpretation asserts that the existing hardening of the hearts of the Israelites only pertains to partial Israel and will continue until the finish of this age. They believe that the Israelites with hardened hearts will turn to Christ at the end of the age and accept salvation, because of God's faithfulness to fulfill his promises in the covenant that was made with Abraham. It is believed that because of the Abrahamic covenant, even Jews with hardened hearts will accept Jesus as the Messiah, and they will receive the Holy Spirit. Regardless of whether or not this is true, everyone should desire that physical Israel whose hearts were hardened would be saved. Israel was spiritually blinded so that the prophecy of redemption could be fulfilled, which was a blessing and a major sacrifice for all humanity.

4. "All Israel" is also believed by some to mean **the church.** The church consists of the Jews and Gentiles

that have been saved. This view uses replacement theology to equate "all Israel" and "the church." Paul educates us on who is a Jew and who is not a Jew in *Rom. 2:28-29.* He says that one is not a Jew, which is one outwardly; neither is He considered to be circumcised just because of what he does to his flesh outwardly. One is a Jew that is a Jew inwardly, and circumcision is of the heart and in the spirit. One is considered to be circumcised if their praise is not of men, but of God. God deserves all glory and praise. Moreover, in *Rom. 9:6-7,* Paul said, that they are NOT all Israel, which are of Israel; neither because they are Abraham's seed, are they all children. This clearly states that election requires more than a certain bloodline. Faith is required to be saved. Because of Jesus' sacrifice on the cross, gentiles were engrafted into Israel.

> *Gal. 3:29* = *And if ye be Christ's, then are ye Abraham's seed, and heirs according to the promise.*

Believing Gentiles were saved before the coming of Christ by God's grace and through their faith in the coming Messiah. Man is not justified by their works of the Law *(Gal. 2:16).* Abraham just believed in God, and he was considered righteous *(Gal. 4:3).*

C. Does "All Israel", In Rom. 11:26, Include "All Zionist?"

Zionism and Judaism are not the same things. The Jewish faith and Zionism have totally different viewpoints, ideas, beliefs, and values. Jewish people have existed for thousands of years, and the Zionist movement was established approximately one hundred years ago. Jews never desired to end their exile and establish independent political sovereignty.

Judaism involves the study and fulfillment of the commandments of the Torah. Zionism is a political movement or government, whose efforts brought thousands of Jews from around the world back to their ancient homeland in the Middle East, and reestablished Israel as the central location for Jewish identity.

The Zionist movement created the Israeli state with the main objective to change the nature of the Jewish people from that of a religious group of people to a political movement. The Jewish people opposed this from the start. Much of the world thinks that the Zionists represent the entire Jewish populace. Jewish people never aspired or selected them to lead their people. Jews have accused Zionists of deceiving many using fear, fraud, and fake publicity. The Jewish faith and the Torah Law of the Jewish people forbid them to have their own state while waiting for the return of the Messiah. God gave the Jews the Holy Land thousands of years ago.

Nonetheless, sin caused it to be taken from them, resulting in their exile. They aim to wait for the Messiah to bring them together ending their exile. The Messiah will also bring about worldwide peace with humanity and all will serve Him. The Zionist state is not a Jewish state; hence, "All Israel" in *Rom. 11:26,* does not mean or include "All Zionist."

D. *The Salvation of God's Chosen People*

Many have wondered why Israel is called God's chosen people. The Lord loves Israel and kept the oath or covenant of love with Abraham and his seed. God promised Israel's forefathers, that He would bring them out of bondage and redeem them from slavery and the power of Pharaoh, the king of Egypt. God chose Israel out of His love. [37]

God chose the nation of Israel to be the line of descents from which Jesus the Savior would be born *(John 3:16).* God promised that He would send the Messiah after the fall of Adam and Eve when man transgressed from God *(Gen. 3).* God promised that the Messiah would come from the lineage of Abraham, Isaac, and Jacob *(Gen. 12:1-3).* Jesus had to come from some nation of people, and God chose Israel. God's reason for choosing the nation of Israel wasn't solely in order to produce our Messiah. He wanted Israel to teach others about Him as a nation of priests, prophets, and missionaries to the world. Israel was not totally successful with the task, but God foreknew this. Nevertheless, God's ultimate purpose for Israel (bringing the Messiah into the world) was fulfilled through the birth of Jesus.[32&37]

Gen. 12:2 tells us that Abraham's descendants are a blessed chosen people. Jesus was born humbly in a stable and rode into Jerusalem on a donkey. However, the Jews were expecting the Messiah to be a great military and political king that would save them as a nation. They failed to recognize Him as the King of kings, who restored the nation and still saves nations. They expected a different Messiah that would come and fulfill the Old Testament prophecies, reinstate their independence, bring them peace/prosperity, and judge their enemies *(Matt. 21:1-11)*. God allowed Jews to experience hardened hearts that prevented them from understanding that Jesus is our Messiah.[37]

Some lack faith in the prophecy being fulfilled regarding the restoration of the Jews because many of them are unbelievers or atheist. Scripture says that we will see the fig tree putting forth fruit or leaves. The Jews in Jerusalem numbered about 550 in 1827, nearly 600,000 by 2005, and currently over 5 million in Israel (and counting).

Prophets such as Micah and Isaiah talk about a time where Israel will see peace and joy. This prophecy is expected to be fulfilled during the Millennial Kingdom period. During this one-thousand years, Jesus will reign, Israel will be blessed, and their enemies will be judged *(Micah 4:2-4; Isa. 32:17-18, 40:1-2, 61:7, 10)*. Judaism looks forward to the ethnic, national, and political salvation of the nation of Israel. They care less about the salvation of individuals. Judaism teaches that when one sins, that they must regret their sins, ask God to forgive them and make amends. Furthermore, they teach that God will pardon them if they are sincere when they are regretful.[37]

In Judaism, there is no major teaching regarding the afterlife, heaven, hell, or what results from God's forgiveness (other than earthly blessings). Some Jews may believe in the afterlife but will attest that the Old Testament Writings do not describe what that is like. The good people will live with God, and the evil people will not. There is a disagreement with Jews regarding the subject of a literal or physical resurrection. Their Scriptures focus more on the earthly life instead of our eternal life or after death. An eternal afterlife with God is promised to those that are faithful believers on earth and not to all Jews as a nation. It is offered to them that depend on the sacrifice of Jesus instead of their own works. Christians believe that we are totally dependent on the sacrifice of Jesus for salvation.

In *Rom. 9:6-8*, we learn that children of the flesh are not considered to be children of God, regardless of whether or not they are descents of Abraham. Even if they come from

Abraham's bloodline, if they do not worship the God of
Abraham, they are not considered to be children of God. *Gal.
3:7* promises that even gentiles with faith in Jesus, are
accepted as children of God. If any man is in Christ, then they
are thought to be Abraham's seed (engrafted into Israel), and
heir according to the Abrahamic covenant.

Gal. 3:28 = *There is neither Jew nor Greek, there is neither
bond nor free, there is neither male nor female: for ye
are all one in Christ Jesus.*

Eph. 2:11-13 = *Wherefore remember, that ye being in time
past Gentiles in the flesh, who are called
Uncircumcision by that which is called the
Circumcision in the flesh made by hands; That at that
time ye were without Christ, being aliens from the
commonwealth of Israel, and strangers from the
covenants of promise, having no hope, and without God
in the world: But now in Christ Jesus ye who sometimes
were far off are made nigh by the blood of Christ.*

Believers become fellow citizens with the saints of Israel,
through Jesus *(Eph. 2:19)*. Those that refuse redemption
through Jesus, even if they are a native Jews from Israel, can't
expect their names to be listed in the Lamb's Book of Life
(Matt. 21:43). The kingdom of God is taken from Jews that
reject Him and given to a believing spiritual nation that serves
Him *(Matt. 21:43)*.

> *1 Pet. 2:9-10* = *ye are a chosen Generation, a royal
> priesthood, an holy nation, a peculiar*

*people; that ye should shew forth the
praises of him who hath called you out
of darkness into his marvellous light:
Which in time past were not a people,
but are now the people of God: which
had not obtained mercy, but now have
obtained mercy.*

Unbelievers that come from Abraham's seed may be hereditarily from Israel, but they are not considered to be a part of "Israel," which God speaks of in ***Rom. 11:26***, where He proclaims that ALL Israel shall be saved. Believers are the true Israel that march to Zion and receive salvation.

The New Testament writers explain how the Old Testament points to Jesus fulfilling the Law. Christians focus more on Jesus and his fulfillment of the Law, whereas Jews concentrate more on keeping the Law ***(Luke 24:27; John 14:6; Matt. 26:28; John 3:16; John 3:18)***.[33&37]

Heb. 10:1-10 describes how Jesus was the way to salvation even in Old Testament times. The Old Testament animal sacrifices were a reminder of their sin. The blood of bulls and goats could not redeem us; therefore, Jesus had to come to reconcile man back to God. Before the coming of Jesus, they still needed to have faith in a righteous and gracious God ***(Rom. 4:3-8)***.

Rom. 4:3-8 = *For what saith the scripture? Abraham believed God, and it was counted unto him for righteousness. Now to him that worketh is the reward not reckoned of grace,* *but of debt. But to him that worketh not, but believeth on him that justifieth the ungodly, his faith is counted for righteousness. Even as David also describeth the blessedness of the man, unto whom God imputeth righteousness without works, Saying, Blessed are they whose iniquities are forgiven, and whose sins are covered. Blessed is the man to whom the Lord will not impute sin.*

Heb. 1:1-2 = *God, who at sundry times and in divers manners spake in time past unto the fathers by the prophets, Hath in these last days spoken unto us by his Son, whom he hath appointed heir of all things, by whom also he made the worlds;*

Consider **Romans 11:25-32.**

Rom. 11:25-36 = *For I would not, brethren, that ye should be ignorant of this mystery, lest ye should be wise in your own conceits; that blindness in part is happened to Israel, until the fulness of the Gentiles be come in. And so all Israel shall be saved: as it is written, There shall come out of Sion the Deliverer, and shall turn away ungodliness from Jacob: For this is my covenant unto them, when I shall take away their sins. As concerning the gospel, they are enemies for your sakes: but as touching the election, they are beloved for the fathers' sakes. For the gifts and calling of God are without repentance. For as ye in times past have not believed God, yet have now obtained mercy through their unbelief: Even so have these also now not believed, that through your mercy they also may obtain mercy. For God hath concluded them all in unbelief, that he might have mercy upon all. O the depth of the riches both of the wisdom and knowledge of God! how unsearchable are his judgments, and his ways past finding out! For who hath known the mind of the Lord? or who hath been his counsellor? Or who hath first given to him, and it shall be recompensed unto him again? For of him, and through him, and to him, are all things: to whom be glory for ever. Amen.*

Some think that there will be a national restoration or national salvation of Israel. The Scripture signifies Israel's blindness, hardness, and the judgment from God as a result. God redefines Israel (thanks to our Savior and Lord, Jesus) to be like an olive tree where the root of the tree represents Abraham's Covenant (the unilateral covenant that Yahweh-Jesus made with Abraham). The olive tree is made up of the people of Yahweh (which is now made up of both the remnant of Jews and the believing Gentiles). The Jews within the olive tree (Israel redefined) are not totally inclusive of all Jews. Some of the branches of the tree have been broken off. The branches that have been broken off represent the ethnic Israelite Jews that hardened their hearts against God and reject Jesus. The gentiles were originally like a wild branch that has now been grafted into the tree. Therefore, the believing gentiles now share in the promises that God made with Israel. Hence, when God says that all of Israel will be saved, He means that all believing Gentiles and believing Jews shall have their names found in the Lamb's Book of Life and will be saved from the damnation of the lake of fire.[37]

There is a partial hardening that happened to Israel and continues until the fullness of the Gentiles have come in *(Rom. 11:25)*. The **hardening** is not partial. The hardening has happened in part to Israel. The remnant is not hardened.

Those that were chosen (the elect Israelites) obtain salvation, and the rest were hardened *(Rom. 11:7)*.[37]

There is a saved remnant according to **Rom. 11:5**. Paul stated that without the hardening of Israel, there would be no gentile salvation. Israel's hardening brought about the salvation of the Gentiles, the destruction of Jerusalem in AD 70, and full confirmation of the New Covenant.[37]

God continues to allow the Jews to remain hardened as the elect Gentiles are gradually grafted or transplanted into the olive tree. The Old Testament does not reveal this. Paul calls this a mystery revealed. God brings Gentiles and Jews together in a relationship of oneness. Initially, the Gentiles were called "Uncircumcised." They were separate from Christ, excluded from the Israel, strangers to the covenant of promise, and without God *(Eph. 2:11-12)*. But now, by the blood of Christ, the Gentiles that were far from God are brought near. God has torn down the walls that divided the Jews from the Gentiles. Both groups are now reconciled in one body through the cross and by the grace of God. This holds true for both believing Jews and Gentiles.[37]

Initially, the word "Israel" referred to the twelve tribes of Israel, the seed of Abraham through Jacob's twelve sons (Reuben, Simeon, Levi, Judah, Issachar, Zebulun, Benjamin, Dan, Naphtali, Gad, Asher, and of course, Joseph). During contemporary times, Israel (the place) comprised mainly of the tribe of Judah, which has been bombarded by Zionists. Zionists are known to generally hate Muslims and Jews, and they practice what is called apartheid. Before Zionism, Jews and the Palestinians were like brothers. Zionism is thought to be a secret society that took control. Zionists are considered to be apostate Jews. The word apostate means those who have turned against God. Many apostate Jews practice demonology, luciferianism, or hidden knowledge exercises.

Some of them are believed to plan an implementation of the Noahide laws that will involve the decapitation of Christians or beheading of Christians. It is common for them to consider the confession of Jesus as Lord to be blaspheming and punishable by death. According to Biblical prophecy, they will kill Christians for the same reason that Jesus was killed. Jesus will save the tribe of Judah at Armageddon, but He will not save the Zionist Jews, who do not worship the God of Abraham, Isaac, and Jacob. All who belong to Christ are thought to be Abraham's descendants and joint heirs with Jesus *(Gal. 3:29)*. Hence, the elect Gentiles and the elect Jews will be saved having their names in the Lamb's Book of Life. Remember, all are NOT Israel just because they are from the nation of Israel.[1,2,37,&42]

Chapter 10

GOD'S FOREKNOWLEDGE - FORESIGHT

In previous chapters, we have already elaborated on the doctrine of foreknowledge. Nevertheless, in this chapter, let us consider two things about "Foreknowledge":

   (1) The Meaning of the Term or It's definition

   (2) The Scriptural Scope of Foreknowledge

"Foreknowledge" is knowing about something or being aware of something before it happens. God's knowledge is infinite. Therefore, God's foreknowing ability allows Him to love mankind prior to our existence. Even before the foundation of this world, God declared us to be His own and intimately knew man. Foresight or foreknowledge allows God to show man affection in past eternity, and God's love is everlasting. He knew the fate of man before He even created Adam and Eve.[20]

  If God was NOT omniscient, then He could NOT be God. If Jehovah is NOT God, then there is NO God. He that believes that there is NO GOD is considered to be an "ATHIEST."[36]

But there is a God, who has absolute foreknowledge. Because He loves us, He gave man a free-will. Love would not be love without making a free-will choice to love. God does not force us to love Him or to serve Him. God is not a tyrant that enslaves elect men, commands them to serve Him, then mandates that they accept Jesus as Lord *(see: 1 Pet. 1)*.[36]

Yet, some believe that God predestined men without considering whether or not they would accept the Gospel and then blesses them with the gift of faith, forcing them to become a believer. This is absurd because it would mean that God placed a mandate on those whom he predestined to serve him and forces them to love Him. God did not even force Satan to continue serving Him, although He had foreknowledge of Satan's rebellion and his convincing one-third of the angels to rebel as well.

Satan's followers also had free-will options to either continue serving God or transgress and serve His adversary. Satan was called Lucifer while he was in the will of God. One great thing about God is that, in addition to being omniscient and having prescience, He is omnipotent or all-powerful. However, He does not have to use His power to manipulate and control men. God infallibly foreknows what man will do beforehand. So, when someone does evil, God uses it for good

(Gen. 50:20). Although God has fore-knowledge because He is omniscient and omnipotent, He has still blessed us with free-will out of His grace.[36]

Relevant Scriptural References:

Acts 2:23 = Him, being delivered by the determinate counsel and foreknowledge of God, ye have taken, and by wicked hands have crucified and slain:

Rom. 8:29 = For whom he did foreknow, he also did predestinate to be conformed to the image of his Son, that he might be the firstborn among many brethren.

Rom. 11:2 = God hath not cast away his people which he foreknew. Wot ye not what the scripture saith of Elias? how he maketh intercession to God against Israel, saying, . . .

1 Pet. 1:2 = Elect according to the foreknowledge of God the Father, through sanctification of the Spirit, unto obedience and sprinkling of the blood of Jesus Christ: Grace unto you, and peace, be multiplied.

Chapter 11

ADOPTION INTO GOD'S FAMILY

In the Greek usage outside of the Bible from Pindar and Herodotus, the word "adoption" means "an adopted son." According to the Encarta Dictionary, "adoption" is a formal legal process of becoming a parent of a child. The word "adoption" (*huiothesias*) also means the placement of a son to someone to whom it does not naturally belong. By law, the adopted person has the same privileges, benefits, position, responsibilities, and obligations as a natural-born son. In other words, "adoption" is the benefit of being united with Jesus, sharing son-ship with Him as joint-heirs, and having rights of being included in God's family. (See the Father/Son relationship example in *Hos. 11*).[22&23]

In the Bible, *Eph. 5:1* suggests that we should be imitators of God, as beloved children. Adoption is a privilege for us who are justified by faith in Jesus to be united with Christ. Gentile believers are adopted as God's children and

admitted into His family.   We are made joint heirs with our
Redeemer, Jesus the Christ.

> ***Rom. 8:14-23*** = *For as many as are led by the Spirit of
> God, they are the sons of God. For ye have not
> received the spirit of bondage again to fear; but ye
> have received the Spirit of adoption, whereby we cry,
> Abba, Father. The Spirit itself beareth witness with our
> spirit, that we are the children of God: And if children,
> then heirs; heirs of God, and joint-heirs with Christ; if
> so be that we suffer with him, that we may be also
> glorified together. For I reckon that the sufferings of
> this present time are not worthy to be compared with
> the glory which shall be revealed in us. For the earnest
> expectation of the creature waiteth for the
> manifestation of the sons of God. For the creature was
> made subject to vanity, not willingly, but by reason of
> him who hath subjected the same in hope, Because the
> creature itself also shall be delivered from the bondage
> of corruption into the glorious liberty of the children of
> God. For we know that the whole creation groaneth
> and travaileth in pain together until now. And not only
> they, but ourselves also, which have the firstfruits of the
> Spirit, even we ourselves groan within ourselves,
> waiting for the adoption, to wit, the redemption of our
> body.*

Adoption is distinguished from justification and
regeneration. Regeneration refers to being spiritually reborn
into God's family. Justification is a legal blessing. Adoption
is a familial/relational blessing and refers to being included in
a family that you were not born into. Due to the adoption of
Christians, we have the freedom to relate to Jehovah God as

our Father, to Jesus as our brother/co-heir, and to the Holy
Spirit as our Leader.[37]

More About Adoption:

- Adoption was orchestrated by God.

  John 1:11-13 = *He came unto his own, and his own
  received him not. But as many as received him, to them
  gave he power to become the sons of God, even to them
  that believe on his name: Which were born, not of
  blood, nor of the will of the flesh, nor of the will of man,
  but of God.*

- God foreknew which believers were individually
  predestined for adoption.

  Eph. 1:4-6 = *According as he hath chosen us in him
  before the foundation of the world, that we should be
  holy and without blame before him in love: having
  predestinated us unto the adoption of children by Jesus
  Christ to himself, according to the good pleasure of his
  will, to the praise of the glory of his grace, wherein he
  hath made us accepted in the beloved.*

- God sent the Holy Spirit into the hearts of the believers
  because we are adopted, children.

  Gal. 4:4-7 = *But when the fulness of the time was come,
  God sent forth his Son, made of a woman, made under
  the law, To redeem them that were under the law, that
  we might receive the adoption of sons. And because ye
  are sons, God hath sent forth the Spirit of his Son into
  your hearts, crying, Abba, Father. Wherefore thou art
  no more a servant, but a son; and if a son, then an heir
  of God through Christ.*

- God must discipline Christians as His children for our own good just as a natural parent needs to discipline their natural-blood children.

> ***Heb. 12:5-11*** *= And ye have forgotten the exhortation which speaketh unto you as unto children, My son, despise not thou the chastening of the Lord, nor faint when thou art rebuked of him: For whom the Lord loveth he chasteneth, and scourgeth every son whom he receiveth. If ye endure chastening, God dealeth with you as with sons; for what son is he whom the father chasteneth not? But if ye be without chastisement, whereof all are partakers, then are ye bastards, and not sons. Furthermore we have had fathers of our flesh which corrected us, and we gave them reverence: shall we not much rather be in subjection unto the Father of spirits, and live? For they verily for a few days chastened us after their own pleasure; but he for our profit, that we might be partakers of his holiness. Now no chastening for the present seemeth to be joyous, but grievous: nevertheless afterward it yieldeth the peaceable fruit of righteousness unto them which are exercised thereby.*

"Adoption" is also discussed in Scripture in ***Rom. 9:4.***

Believers in Jesus are adopted sons, not fearful slaves.

Adoption is included in the blessings of salvation.

> ***Rom. 8:23*** *= And not only they, but ourselves also, which have the firstfruits of the Spirit, even we ourselves groan within ourselves, waiting for the adoption, to wit, the redemption of our body.*

This is our blessed hope *(Rom. 8:24-25)*. The adopted children of God are treated as new persons upon conversion. All of their old debts and obligations connected with the old creature were eradicated. Additionally, they become heirs to all of the inheritance of their new Father by the right of the Law. The adopted children get the benefit of enjoying the same privileges as natural-born children.

As descendants of Adam and Eve, we are all affected by the power of sin and guilt. Because of this, we were born into and responsible for sin. God took believers out of Adam's family and adopted us into His everlasting family. Through the blood of Jesus, we are released from the debt of sin (which is death) because Jesus paid the debt for us in full on the cross at Mount Calvary. As adopted children of the Most-High God, Christians have legal rights within our new family of God *(Rom. 5:12-21, 8:14-23; 1 John 3:1; Rev. 21:7)*. And God has complete rights over believers because we are His possessions since we were bought by the Lamb of God (Jesus) for the steep price of His sacrificial life.[38]

When believers possess faith in Jesus, we received a "spirit of adoption." Afterward, believers are allowed into God's presence. Subsequently, the Holy Spirit enables the believers to call God, "Father" *(Rom. 8:15),* and Scripture instructs us to call NO man father other than our heavenly Father *(Matt. 23:9)*. Jesus taught this concept to His disciples.

Prior to the first coming of Christ, even the Jewish did not call God, "Father." The Holy Spirit assures our own spirit that we are God's children *(Rom. 8:15)*. Before becoming a child of God, man is considered a slave to sin and may fear God as a result of their unrighteousness. The Holy Spirit that dwells within believers releases us from fear so that we can experience peace and intimacy with our heavenly Father *(Rom. 8:15)*.[38]

We are God's children in two ways. First, as adopted children of our heavenly Father, we are co-heirs along with Jesus *(John 17:24; 1 Cor. 3:21-23; Gal. 4:7)*. Secondly, we are also His children by the new birth or being born again *(John 1:1; 3:5; 1 John 3:1-3)*. Both are accomplished through Jesus and the Holy Spirit.[38]

Children of God receive spiritual blessings in this life and the eternal afterlife *(Eph. 1:3; 2 Tim. 2:12; 1 Pet. 4:13, 5:10)*. Unfortunately, believers may also share in Christ's sorrow *(John 15:20; Col. 1:24; 2 Tim. 3:12; 1 Pet. 4:12)*. Through the Holy Spirit, we are empowered to be more like Christ, who still submitted to God's will when facing the torture of the cross.[37]

> *Luke 22:42* = *Saying, Father, if thou be willing, remove this cup from me: nevertheless not my will, but thine, be done.*

Chapter 12

DOCTRINE OF REGENERATION

Regeneration is a way of God that offers new life to mankind. Regeneration means to reform or restructure, and goes hand in hand with sanctification and justification. When a believer gets born again, they become a new creature or new creation. They are born again to a new life. This process is considered to be regeneration *(2 Cor. 5:17; John 3:3–6)*. The process of rebirth does not occur as a result of the believer's works of righteousness but is a gift from God that is given according to His mercy. God saves us by the cleansing of regeneration and renewing of the Holy Ghost *(Titus 3:4-7)*.[20&22]

Jesus taught the vital importance of being born again, or the new birth, when He said, *'Truly, truly I say to you, unless one is born again, he cannot see the kingdom of God'* *(John 3:5)*. Jesus informs us that it is not enough for people to do good works. Being born again is essential for salvation.

All humans are born from their mother's womb. Then we are born again when we become believers in Jesus and confess Him as Lord *(Rom. 10:10).*

Man must be recreated on the inside to inherit God's kingdom. An unbeliever needs to be transformed into a new life through the intervention of the Holy Spirit. Regeneration is where God supernaturally creates a new heart in a new believer, fills them with the Holy Spirit, and blesses them with eternal life. As we learn in *John 6:44*, no one comes to Christ unless the Father draws him first. The Lord enlightens and opens man up to understand His truths *(Acts 16:14; John 3:6-8; Eph. 1:17–18).* When someone is regenerated, they are supernaturally recreated in Christ's image. In the beginning, man was created in God's image. However, as a result of the "The Fall" of Adam and Eve, man must be recreated or regenerated. By the death of Jesus on the cross, man can be saved from the damnation of the second death.[33]

The words "Rebirth" and "Regeneration" are interchangeable. The rebirth of a person causes them to be considered "born again" or called a "born again Christian." To be born again is different from our initial birth where we are born into sin from childbirth. The rebirth is a spiritual and heavenly birth that brings eternal spiritual life. Our first birth is a birth into spiritual death due to the inherited sin of "the fall." In man's natural state from birth, he is dead in sin until he is regenerated by having faith in Jesus *(Eph. 2:1-8)*. When people are regenerated, they are filled with the Holy Spirit. This infilling of the Holy Spirit causes the regenerated person to strive to live holy as Jesus did. We become new creatures and take on the divine nature of Christ. This does not occur due to man's goodness or good works. It happens because of God's love, grace, and mercy that is shown to believers. Rebirth is a free gift and a part of the "salvation pack," in conjunction with sealing *(Eph. 1:14),* adoption *(Gal. 4:5),* reconciliation *(2 Cor. 5:18-20),* etc. Being born again is sometimes expressed as "being born from above." Through regeneration, man becomes a new creature that is spiritually alive as a result of faith in the Lord, Jesus *(John 3:6-7; Eph. 2:1; 1 Pet. 1:23; John 1:13; 1 John 3:9, 4:7, 5:1-18).*[32]

All humans need to be regenerated because unless we accept Jesus as our Lord and Savior, we are not considered to be God's children *(John 1:12-13).* Before salvation, all were degenerate, and after salvation, we are regenerated *(Eph. 2:3; Rom. 5:18-20).* Regeneration brings us peace, new life and eternal son-ship *(Rom. 5:1; Titus 3:5; 2 Cor. 5:17; John 1:1-21; Gal. 3:26).* Regeneration begins the process of sanctification. The sanctification process is where we start to become more like Christ *(Rom. 8:28-30).* Regeneration or the new birth (being born again), is the process cure for total depravity and is unique to Christianity. Man's good works, according to God's Law, can NOT justify him *(Rom. 3:20)*. Regeneration of the heart is essential for justification-salvation *(Gal. 2:20)*.[32]

> ***Rom. 6:3-5*** = *Know ye not, that so many of us as were baptized into Jesus Christ were baptized into his death? Therefore we are buried with him by baptism into death: that like as Christ was raised up from the dead by the glory of the Father, even so we also should walk in newness of life. For if we have been planted together in the likeness of his death, we shall be also in the likeness of his resurrection:*

Salvation is NOT acquired from the application of water to one's physical flesh. Regeneration is sometimes seen as a part of the "Ordo salutis" or the *"order of salvation"* in Christian theology. It is a work of God in the believer's life *(Eph. 2:4)*. The Greek noun "rebirth" or "regeneration" (Ancient Greek: παλιγγενεσία *palingenesia*) appears twice in the New Testament *(Matt. 19:28; Titus 3:5)*. Regeneration represents an expansive theme of recreation and spiritual rebirth. It includes the concept of being born again where the new believer becomes different or a changed creature *(John 3:3-8; 1 Pet. 1:3)*.

Mankind was created to praise, worship, exalt, and glorify God. The original fall of man prevents mankind from doing so. The fall also keeps mankind from fulfilling their

God-given purposes without regeneration. God purposed the salvation plan through his Son, in order for men to regain their ability to serve Him as they should. God redeems us through His love, grace, power, and perfect justice by way of Jesus. Regeneration is God's Holy Spirit working in the souls of mankind.

The Old Testament indicates that regeneration is a way of circumcising or softening unholy hardened hearts *(Deut. 30:6; Ezek. 36:26)*. God writes His Law on man's heart *(Jer. 31:33)*. The New Testament describes regeneration as a person becoming a born-again creation and being brought from death to life *(2 Cor. 5:17; John 3:3; Rom. 6:13)*. They are called out of satanic darkness and bought into the light of God *(1 Pet. 2:9)*. During the regeneration process, God changes the spirit of the believer, and the spirit affects their soul.[32]

After one is regenerated, they are converted. Regeneration is an act of God, while conversion is an act of the believer that involves their consciousness. The soul consists of the mind, emotions, and one's will, and conversion happens to the soul at the beginning of the believer's changed lifestyle, where they begin to live holy. Without regeneration, all of mankind would remain spiritually blind and dead in sin.[33]

Chapter 13

EXPIATION and PROPITIATION

EXPIATION and **PROPITIATION** (pronounced = *ex pee ay' shuhn* and *proh pih tee ay' shuhn*) are synonymous terms that are used by Christian theologians to define the meaning of Christ's death on the cross relating to God and His believing children. Propitiation relates to redemption or reconciliation, which is by Christ's sacrificial death for our sins *(Rom. 5:9-11; 2 Cor. 5:18-21; Col. 1:19-23)*.

There are also some differences between expiation and propitiation. Expiation focuses more on the removal of the guilt of sin by the payment for the sin that was paid by Jesus at Mount Calvary. On the other hand, propitiation deals more with the forestalling or preventing God's wrath and penalizing mankind for sin.[24&32] Theologians have expressed differences in interpretation regarding the Greek word for propitiation, which is "*hilasmos*" *(see: 1 John 2:2, 4:10)*. A variety of Biblical translations use varied distinctions such as:[23&32]

1. (KJV, NAS) = uses "propitiation"
2. (RSV) = uses "expiation"
3. (NIV, NRSV, compare REB) = "atoning sacrifice for our sins"
4. (TEV) = "means by which our sins are forgiven"
5. Related Greek words in *Matt. 16:22, Luke 18:13, Rom. 3:25, and Heb. 2:17, 8:12, 9:5.*
6. KJV uses various translations of these words: "be merciful," "make reconciliation," "*to be* a propitiation," "the mercy-seat," "be it far from thee," "I will be merciful."

In Greek writings, *hilasmos* meant soothing the anger of the gods. The Septuagint is the earliest Greek translation of the Old Testament. In the Septuagint, the word *hilasmos* appears in:

1. *Lev. 25:9* = in the expression, "day of atonement"
2. *Psalm 130:4* = to assure that God "forgives"
3. *Num. 5:8* = in the expression the "ram of the atonement"
4. *Ezek. 44:27* = as a "sin-offering."
5. *Dan. 9:9* = to show the character traits of God using the plural form of the word to indicate "forgiveness"

God gave mankind refuge and forgives us of our sins. During this course of action, He eradicates the defilement of man's sin. Some consider God to be the one that accepted Jesus' offering for sin. They think that it reduced His anger bringing justice. Others think that God initiated Jesus' sacrifice to provide forgiveness for human sin. They too believe that the sacrifice satisfied God's rile and generated justice.[38]

The Old Testament documents the sacrificial system prior to the birth of Jesus. Men made an attempt at remaining obedient to God's commands. God was merciful, especially on those who practiced particular rituals [i.e. the burnt offering *(Lev. 1:3-17),* the peace offering *(Lev. 3:1-17),* the sin offering *(Lev. 4:1-5:13),* and the guilt offering *(Lev. 5:15-6:6)*]. These did not deal with defiant sins or iniquity that is caused by the **refusal** to obey God *(Num. 15:20-31).* These offerings were purposed for "sin through ignorance" *(Lev. 4:2).* On the annual day of atonement, the sins of the people were forgiven when the high priest sacrificed animals on the altar *(Lev. 16:1-34).*[38]

With grace, God specified what kind of sacrifices that He desired. Remember that even when Abraham was willing to sacrifice his only begotten son, Isaac, God ultimately supplied him with the ram in the bush *(Gen. 22:1-19).* God has consistently remained merciful on sinners by being willing to forgive us even before we sin *(Psalms 78:21-28, 89:28-34; Isa. 65:1-2; Jer. 31:1-3, 31-34; Hos. 6:1-2).* Although God is readily prepared to forgive man of our sins, He also petitions us to confess, repent, and obey His commands.

The New Testament reveals that Jesus did not come to destroy the Old Testament Law, instead, He came to fulfill it

(Matt. 5:17). He came to replace the sacrificial system of old times by being the last necessary sacrificial Lamb on the cross at Mount Calvary. God willingly provided His only begotten Son, Jesus, as this perfect sacrifice. This sacrifice of Christ is sufficient to cover the sins of all of humanity *(Heb. 7:26-28, 9:25-26)*. The sacrifice of the life of Jesus restored the relationship between God and believers. Jesus made it possible for everyone to reconcile with God *(Rev. 13:8)*.[38]

Jehovah God is loving, as well as holy. For this reason, he cannot condone sin. Man must acknowledge the sacrificial offering of the life of Jesus, in order to make amends for their sin and receive redemption. The New Testament confirms the Old Testament's teaching that only through Jesus can we be restored. All Old Testament ritual requirements for sacrifice are replaced by the sacrifice of Jesus. The sacrifice of the only perfect Lamb of God, Jesus, destroyed the need for any additional animal sacrifices. The death of Christ gives mankind an option to confess and repent of our sins, so that we may have our sins forgotten *(Col. 2:14; Heb. 10:14-18)*. We must show our appreciation for God giving us a second chance to experience eternal life with Him. We can show thanks through praise, worship, obedience, service, and sharing the Gospel or Good News with others.[38]

We may deduce that both propitiation (evading the wrath of God), and expiation (taking away the human guilt of sin), are included in the doctrine of the atonement. God, through Jesus, performs expiation/propitiation. The sacrifice of a perfect Lamb of God, Jesus, was needed to satisfy the demands of God's Law. God so loved the world that He gave His only begotten Son, that man may be saved from their sin and damnation *(John 3:16)*.

Chapter 14

THE SANCTIFICATION PROCESS

Sanctification is the process of acquiring holiness, being set apart for a certain use, and being more dedicated to God. "Sanctity" is an ancient religious concept. It is a characteristic of a thing or person that is holy, sacred, and Godly. This word can be used to refer to a thing such as the Ark of the Covenant. It can also be used to describe believers that have been justified through Christ and have received the infilling of God's Holy Spirit. To be sanctified is to be reserved for a special purpose. In Christian theology, sanctification is a state of making someone holy unto God. All believers enter into this state when they are born again of God. It is etymologically from the Latin verb "sanctificare," which in turn, is from the two words, sanctus "holy" and *facere* "to make." **Sanctification is often equated with the spiritual growth in a Christian's life. It is God's will for us.**[24&39]

In ***John 17:16,*** Jesus says, *"They are not of the world, even as I am not of the world,"* . . . *"Sanctify them in the truth: Thy word is truth."* Sanctification is a process that helps a person fulfill their appointed God-given purpose. Believers begin a phase of sanctification after confessing Jesus the Christ as their Lord and Savior.

> ***1 Cor. 1:30*** = *But of him are ye in Christ Jesus, who of God is made unto us wisdom, and righteousness, and sanctification, and redemption:*

There is a separation process, which is eternal and will result in a believer being separated from unbelievers. Believers will eventually go to heaven, while unbelievers will be separated and eventually wind up in the lake of fire. Sanctification is an interrelated part of our salvation and our relation to Christ ***(Heb. 10:10).*** Sanctification is the effect of obedience to God's commands and following His statutes. Believers must continuously strive to be sanctified by growing spiritually throughout our spiritual walk with God while living on earth ***(1 Pet. 1:15; Heb. 12:14).*** The world should benefit from the believer's sanctification since God has given us the assignment of the Great Commission (to spread the Gospel to all nations of the world). [39]

> ***John 17:18-19*** = *As thou hast sent me into the world, even so have I also sent them into the world.*

And for their sakes I sanctify myself, that they also might be sanctified through the truth.

John 10:36 = *Say ye of him, whom the Father hath sanctified, and sent into the world, Thou blasphemest; because I said, I am the Son of God?*

Let's discuss various phases of sanctification:

1. **"Positional Sanctification"** – At salvation, believers are justified and made righteous to the image of Christ. God foreknew us and predestined the elect to become conformed to the image of His Son *(Rom. 8:29)*. This is God's work in us.

2. **"Experiential Sanctification"** – This comes with spiritual maturity. One attempts to be Christ-like. The Holy Spirit within produces Godliness in the believer's life. Progressive sanctification is experiencing the results of our position with Jesus. The Holy Spirit that dwells within believers, empowers them to resist the temptation of sin. A transformation takes place through the renewing of the mind of the believer *(Rom. 12:2)*. Although one makes progress during their sanctification process, they still must expect to face spiritual warfare. Satan opposes sanctification and the Holy Spirit existing in our lives. One must allow God's will to

prevail. Progressive sanctification comes by way of the Holy Spirit so that man becomes righteous and lives by faith *(1 Pet. 1:14-16).*

3. **"Ultimate Sanctification"** - The final stage in the salvation process is the ultimate sanctification of the believer. This is the glorification of the believer. It takes place at the resurrection when the believer will be transformed into their glorified heavenly body that will be holy and in the likeness of the Jesus. The Holy Spirit that dwells within us brings future glorification to the believer. The believer receives a redemption body, an eternal inheritance, and an escape from God's wrath *(Eph. 1:13-14; 1 Cor. 1:22).* Christians are redeemed from the "Penalty" of sin through "Justification," from the "Power" of sin through "Sanctification," and from the "Presence" of sin through "Glorification."

God continues to sanctify believers as we continue to serve Him on earth, spreading the Gospel to help build His kingdom. Consequently, believers are considered to be 'sanctified ones' and called saints. Unbelievers, usually show a worldly behavior that gives a clue to their lack of a spiritual relationship with God. On the other hand, Christian's conduct should bear witness to their salvation due to the sanctification process.

In *1 Thess. 5:23* Paul prayed, *"The God of peace Himself sanctify you wholly; and may your spirit and soul and body be preserved entire, without blame at the coming of our Lord Jesus Christ."* Please understand, the sanctification period may create a new man, but it does not create a perfect man. It is the glorification process that blesses believers with an everlasting separation from sin. Glorification occurs at the end of the sanctification process, which is called "total sanctification." [39]

Chapter 15

GLORIFICATION OF THE BELIEVERS

The word "Glorification" may have several different meanings amongst the various Christian denominations. Since the Bible does NOT support denominationalism, let us consider what glorification means according to non-denominational Christians and Scripture *(1 Cor. 1:12-16)*. There are two events that occur during glorification. One of these is when the elect (all of those whose names are written in the Lamb's Book of Life) become entirely without fault before entering God's kingdom. Secondly, the elect receive new resurrection bodies or celestial bodies.[39]

The first phase of this Christian process involves justification. During the second step, the believer is sanctified. In the third phase, the believer is glorified. *(See: Rom. 8:28-30)* Glorification is the consummation or final step of our salvation. The second stage of Christian development is to exalt God through one's life. Man must decrease so that God may increase. When this is accomplished, other people that come in contact with that Christian can witness that believer's sanctification. They begin to see the characteristics of Jesus in that person. They can actually feel the presence of God (by way of the Holy Spirit) that dwells within the believer. This occurs before the first death while one is still alive on earth.[29&39]

Glorification first involves the believer's sanctification, which improves their morals. The believer is made glorious, holy, and blameless *(2 Thess. 2:13-14; Heb. 2:10-11; Eph. 5:27).* After being justified, one continues the sanctification process that moves from one degree of glory to another until it reaches full glory *(2 Cor. 3:18).*

Glorification is a process where those who are dead in Christ (or dead believers), and those in Christ that will be living at that time, will be called up or caught up in the air with Jesus *(1 Thess. 4:16-17).* They will receive new, glorified, perfect, sinless, celestial bodies. This phase of glorification is the future work of God, where He transforms our terrestrial physical earthly bodies into the new eternal bodies.[39]

> *1 Cor. 15:42-44 = So also is the resurrection of the dead. It is sown in corruption; it is raised in incorruption: It is sown in dishonour; it is raised in glory: it is sown in weakness; it is raised in power: It is sown a natural body; it is raised a spiritual body. There is a natural body, and there is a spiritual body.*

1 Thess. 4:16-17 = *For the Lord himself shall descend from heaven with a shout, with the voice of the archangel, and with the trump of God: and the dead in Christ shall rise first: Then we which are alive and remain shall be caught up together with them in the clouds, to meet the Lord in the air: and so shall we ever be with the Lord.*

Jesus can be considered to be the first fruits of creation since He was the first earthly being to be resurrected from the dead and receive His glorified body *(1 Cor. 15:20).*

1 Cor. 15:51-53 = *Behold, I shew you a mystery; We shall not all sleep, but we shall all be changed, In a moment, in the twinkling of an eye, at the last trump: for the trumpet shall sound, and the dead shall be raised incorruptible, and we shall be changed. For this corruptible must put on incorruption, and this mortal must put on immortality.*

Glorification converts believers, bringing a final removal of sin at the end of this age. It deals with the perfection of the believers once they have received a new sinless, glorified, celestial body. This occurs when the believers are caught up at the time of resurrection (the rapture). The word "glorification" is not found in the Hebrew Old Testament Scripture or the Greek New Testament Scripture. However, the concept of glorification is expressed by the Greek verb *doxazo* [doxavzw] ("glorify") and the noun *doxa* [dovxa] ("glory").

Rom. 8:30 appears, at first sight, to place glorification in the past, but one must consider God's all-knowing, omniscient, foreknowledge characteristics.

> *Rom. 8:30* = *Moreover whom he did predestinate, them he also called: and whom he called, them he also justified: and whom he justified, them he also glorified.*

God is the Alpha and Omega *(Rev. 22:13)*. He is the Beginning and the End (the first and the last). He already knows how our stories will end. In other Scriptures, glorification is referred to in the future tense, such as:

1) something to be sought and hoped for *(Rom. 5:2; Col. 1:27)*

2) to be revealed *(Rom. 8:18; 1 Pet. 5:1)*

3) to be obtained *(2 Thess. 2:14; 2 Tim. 2:10)*

Glorification is fulfilled at the end of the age *(Eph. 5:27; Phil. 3:20-21; Col. 3:4; 2 Thess. 1:10)*. It is accompanied by the resurrection of believers into eternal life and the day of judgment *(1 Cor. 15:43; Rom. 2:5-10; 2 Col. 4:17; 2 Tim. 2:10; 1 Pet. 5:10)*. God prepares us for glory, which we inherit *(Rom. 9:23, 8:17; 1 Cor. 2:9)*.

When the church participates in the glorification process, they experience deliverance and are liberated *(Rom. 8:23; 1 Col. 15:43; Phil. 3:21; Rom. 8:21)*. The new glorified body of the believer is incorruptible, immortal, imperishable, and spiritual *(Rom. 2:7; 1 Cor. 15:43-44)*. Christians will be delivered from the bondage of the corruption of sin and transformed into glorious liberty as children of God *(Rom. 8:21)*. The glorification process allows those whose names are written in the Lamb's Book of Life the opportunity to take part in God's glory upon receiving a new glorified body *(Rom. 5:2; 1 Thess. 2:12; 2 Thess. 2:14; 1 Pet. 5:10)*. The glorified body is immortal, imperishable, blameless, and spiritual.

Chapter 16

PRESERVATION

ETERNAL SECURITY vs. APOSTASY

The word "apostasy' is taken from the Greek word "apostasia." It is the turning away from one's faith or belief in Christ, or when one denounces the one and only true and living God *(1 Titus 1:19)*. The person's heart turns away from Jehovah God *(Heb. 3:13; 2 Pet. 2:20)*. It could be a case where someone renounces Godly beliefs that they previously held. It might be a withdrawal from any type of religion. Apostasy can be an abandonment of one's previous religious practices and rebellion against those beliefs. The person that is guilty of apostasy is an apostate.[24&32]

There are various things that typically occur prior to becoming an apostate:

1. One thinks back to the prior sin that they participated regularly in past time *(Luke 9:62)*. As a result, they sometimes turn from God, and like a dog returning to his own vomit, they are foolish

enough to return to their old sinful ways *(Prov. 26:11)*. Believers should learn from prior mistakes. Scripture warns us with the example of Lot's wife. After leaving Sodom (which represented sin), she looked back at Sodom after God commanded them to leave and not to look back. Because of her disobedience, she was turned into a pillar of salt.

2. Secondly, that person transgresses back *(Heb. 10:38)* because they think that the requirements of Christianity are too demanding for them; therefore, holiness no longer appeals to their heart.

3. Third, the person turns back *(John 6:66)* because they give in to the lusts of the flesh.

4. Fourth, they fatally fall back.

   Isa. 28:13 = *But the word of the LORD was unto them precept upon precept, precept upon precept; line upon line, line upon line; here a little, and there a little; that they might go, and fall backward, and be broken, and snared, and taken).*

Man is not saved based on his good works or his ability to resist sin. However, some fail to maintain a repenting heart and die in their sin because they decide that sin means more to them than their allegiance to God. By their own choice, Satan becomes their god. There are some who have confessed Jesus as Lord and appear to live Christian-like for years. Then they literally decide to sell their souls to Satan for a life of fame, fortune, homosexuality, and/or power, etc. Some placed allegiance with Satan after confessing Jesus as Lord because they allow tribulations to cause them to get so angry with God that they begin to serve the antichrist.

After someone accepts Christ, Satan continues to tempt them. If Satan tempted Jesus, why wouldn't he attempt to persuade all mankind to transgress against God? It is his prime desire to cause believers to turn from God. Christians have a responsibility to resist Satan's temptations. Man's resistance causes Satan to flee by the power of the Holy Spirit that lives within the believer *(James 4:7)*. Man's lack of resistance to sin causes Satan to continue tempting us to perform the same sins repeatedly. Satan's ultimate goal is to steal our souls so that we may spend eternity with him in the lake of fire. Satan desperately yearns to be like God, so since it is God's desire for man to be eternally reconciled back to Him, Satan craves the exact opposite.[32]

A. Once Saved ➔ Always Saved

The word "Salvation" in Hebrew and the Greek means to save, rescue, and deliver. "Salvation" in Hebrew also means "Yeshua," which is another name for Jesus, our Messiah. Some believe that they could lose their salvation because of sin against God. If this was true and all have sinned, this would cause them to bring condemnation upon themselves and begin to lose faith. This controversial question arises, if a person receives God's gift of salvation, will they always remain saved? Or can anyone lose their salvation? This is a much-debated subject amongst Christians.

Do not insult the Spirit of grace with continual sin. Do not attempt to take advantage of God's grace, thinking that because you have accepted Jesus/Yeshua/Salvation, you can deliberately recurrently sin as much as you like. ***Heb. 10:26-27*** warns that if we sin willfully after we have received the knowledge of the truth, there remains no more sacrifice for sins. There will be a fearful judgment and fiery indignation, which shall devour the adversaries. Believers can not only be hearers of God's Word. Although we are not saved based on good works, we must be doers of God's Word, as well as hearers.

> ***Matt. 7:21*** = *Not every one that saith unto me, Lord, Lord, shall enter into the kingdom of heaven; but he that doeth the will of my Father which is in heaven.*

At the time of judgment, many will say to God, Lord, have we not prophesied in thy name? And in thy name, have we not cast out devils? And in thy name, have we done many wonderful works? And God will reply, I never knew you: depart from me, ye that work iniquity. But whosoever that hears God's sayings and does them, He will be like them as a wise man, which built his house upon a rock *(Matt. 7:21-24)*.

Yes, Jesus has paid the price for our sins. Because the price can't be paid with our works, else it could cause the sinner to boast. Nevertheless, we must renew our minds with redemptive thoughts. This helps to purge us of the sin-consciousness that can bring guilt and feelings of unworthiness. Comprehending the eternal result of Jesus' sacrifice for us will change our assessment of ourselves. Knowing who we are in Christ aids in our spiritual growth.

> ***Heb. 9:11-12*** *= But Christ being come an high priest of good things to come, by a greater and more perfect tabernacle, not made with hands, that is to say, not of this building; Neither by the blood of goats and calves, but by his own blood he entered in once into the holy place, having obtained eternal redemption for us.*

Jesus gave His life on the cross with the purpose of being the last needed blood sacrifice for the atonement of man's sin, in a similar way that animals were sacrificed prior to the sacrificial death of Jesus. There was a major difference in the sacrifice of Christ versus the animal sacrifices. That is, the blood of Christ did not just cover the sins of mankind, but it actually blotted them out. If Jesus is your Lord, the blood of Christ blots out past, present, and future sins. Additionally, the sacrifice of Christ was perfect, complete, and eternal. The blood of Jesus cleanses forever. However, does that assure us that it will continue to cleanse someone regardless of their actions?

God has given mankind the gift of "FREE-WILL." When a person confesses Jesus as their Lord, if they change their mind afterward and denounce their allegiance to Christ, are they still covered by the blood of Christ? If believers change their minds and later denounce Jesus as Lord, they are in a sense returning God's gift of redemption. Let us consider the following hypothetical analogy to get a better understanding of this principle. If someone were to give you a new car as a gift and you accept it, you will be capable of driving the new car to get wherever you like.

However, if you return the car that was given to you, you will no longer be able to drive what you no longer have. If that car had been your only means of transportation, you won't be able to drive to your desired destination. Well, Jesus was sent to the cross as a gift to us from Jehovah God, and He is our only means of getting to heaven. Therefore, should we deny Christ as Lord even after accepting the Gift, then we lose our only means for eternal life and being spared from damnation.

The Holy Spirit that dwells within Christians is responsible for "keeping us" *(2 Titus 1:14)*; so some may say that denying God would not be possible after accepting God.

God is a gentleman (again, not a slave driver or tyrant) and does not force Himself upon anyone. God, Christ, and the Holy Spirit are one.

Hence, if someone decides that they do not want the Holy Spirit to dwell within them anymore after accepting Christ, the Holy Spirit has the power to depart from that person just as easily as He entered. God warns us to be faithful until death *(Rev. 2:10-11).*

> ***Matt. 10:22*** *= And ye shall be hated of all men for my name's sake: but he that **endureth to the end shall be saved.***

The Holy Spirit is also omnipotent or all-powerful and can do all things (including departing from the dwelling place of a person who denounces Jesus as Lord). Consider all of the Biblical Scripture where demons were cast out of the people that were possessed. Those demonic spirits lived within that possessed person and later departed. Why then, would one think that the Holy Spirit would be less capable of departing from a person's dwelling after residing in them?

Some declare that if one rebukes Jesus after confessing Him as Lord, then they never truly accepted Him as their Lord in the first place. Some may wonder, when the person confessed Jesus as Lord, did their heart sincerely mean what their lips confessed? Or were they confessing Jesus as Lord openly before man out of the fear of being eternally damned?

Personally, I knew a man that admitted to confessing Jesus as Lord in church for the sole purpose of getting appointed as a trustee in order to get close to the collection plates. He eventually started his own business with stolen church funds. The business was initially very financially successful. Not to my surprise, it failed shortly after its success.

Consider Lucifer before his fall. Lucifer was initially a faithful servant to God. He would have experienced eternal life with God had he not allowed his free-will to cause him to desire to be like the Most-High God, Jehovah *(Isa. 14:14)*. What's worse, out of his jealousy and pride, he decided that he would take over God's throne. As a result of his free-will transgression against God, he was cast out of heaven like lightning *(Luke 10:18)*. His betrayal will also secure him an eternal place in the lake of fire *(Rev. 19:20; 20:10)*.

The significant point to remember is that everyone is in need of redemption. By nature, we are all born into sin or guilty of sin. The redemption of Christ has bought us liberty from guilt and justifies us freely by His grace *(Rom. 3:24)*. The benefits of redemption include eternal life *(Rev. 5:9-10),* righteousness *(Rom. 5:17),* adoption as a child of God *(Gal. 4:5),* forgiveness of sins *(Eph. 1:7),* freedom from the law's curse *(Gal. 3:13),* deliverance from the bondage of sin *(Titus 2:14; 1 Pet. 1:14-18),* infilling of the Holy Ghost *(1 Cor. 6:19-20),* and peace *(Col. 1:18-20),* etc. To be redeemed is to experience reconciliation by the blood of Christ through faith. Jesus provided the ransom or paid the price for our release from sin and its consequences *(Matt. 20:28; 1 Tim. 2:6).* His death was in exchange for our life *(Col. 1:14).*

Many come to the church altars and confess Jesus. Not all that come to the Lord remain. They may test the water to see if it feels good to them, and if not, they find different water that they think is more comfortable and that they like better. The sad thing is that they are looking for better water when they already had the best. Christ is the living water, and whoever drinks of His water shall thirst no more *(John 4:11-14).* Some of those that were called by God were blown away because they were like chaff. They did not wholeheartedly believe and accept Jesus as Lord. They may have only wanted a Savior and NOT a Lord. Many times, this occurs because they still want to be their own Lord and only desire Jesus to save them from damnation.

Some renounce the religious profession that they once confessed and expose the inward apostasy of their heart. Some turn from Christ because they cannot bear the Holy Doctrine. The Bible was not written with intentions to please man's flesh. God's intention was to save man from his sin. Don't expect God to modify His statutes in order that men can be comfortable with their sin.

Christians understand apostasy to be a willful falling away from, or rebellion against, Christian truth. Apostasy is the rejection of Christ by one who has been a Christian. Some believe that this is Biblically impossible. Apostasy is the antonym of conversion. It is a de-conversion. The Greek noun *apostasia* means rebellion, abandonment, state of apostasy, or defection. Although it is found only twice in the New Testament *(Acts 21:21; 2 Thess. 2:3),* the idea of apostasy is found throughout Scripture *(Josh. 22:22; 2 Chron. 29:19)*.

Apostasy is also thought of as the heart turning away from God and righteousness *(Jer. 17:5-6; Ezek. 3:20)*. In the Old Testament, we find Israel breaking covenant relationship with God through the disobedience of the Law *(Jer. 2:19)*. The Israelites became immoral and even began to worship false gods *(Judges 2:19; Dan. 9:9-11)*. The Hebrew root "swr" is used to picture those who have ceased to follow God *(1 Sam. 15:11)*. In *Matt. 7:24-27,* Jesus clearly expresses the dangers of hearing His Word and disobeying it.

Preservation is faith-based and grounded in God's counsel/guidance. It passes through believers in Christ and assists in the spread of the Scriptures. Apostasy is a Biblical concept or a theological term. However, it is not actually a Biblical term or word that you will find in the KJV Bible. Amongst Christians, you may find some deliberation regarding the issues of apostasy and salvation. Some believe that once one confesses Jesus as Lord, they are forever saved. While others profess that because of our God-given free-will, we have an option to denounce Jesus even after accepting Him as Lord. Some think that any who fall away from Christ were never saved in the first place. In other words, they may have "believed" for some period of time, but were never regenerated.

Again, many understand that Biblical warnings against apostasy are NOT to be ignored because God gives Christians the freedom to reject Him and salvation. God also warns us NOT to place confidence in the flesh *(Phil. 3:3)*. As long as men live within their terrestrial earthly flesh, we are capable of transgression.

Even believers will fall into sin against God until we receive our glorified, celestial, heavenly bodies *(1 Cor. 15:35-49)*. Thankfully (glory to God), if believers sin, we can confess/repent of our sin because we have an advocate with the Father, Jesus Christ the righteous, who is faithful and just to forgive us of our sin *(1 John 1:9, 2:1)*. There are three concepts of sin (chief sin from which all other sin is derived):

1. **UNBELIEF** – One has a lack of faith or a loss of trust in God (Adam and Eve lost trust in God by way of the serpent).

2. **PRIDE** - Where a person is proud, and they have a foolishly and irrationally corrupt sense of their own personal value, status, or accomplishments. It is an inwardly directed emotion. They exalt themselves higher than they ought.

3. **SELF WILL** - Self-will is part of our fleshly nature, and it causes one to strive to make themselves the center of their own motivations. Self-will causes the desire to pull away from God and deny justice in order to advance their own carnal drives. One does what they want to do, rather than what God wills.

Certainly, God is faithful and just to forgive us of our sins if we confess/repent of that sin. On the other hand, there is an unpardonable sin. Every sin and blaspheme may be forgiven by God, but the blasphemy against the Holy Spirit never gets forgiveness and can cause eternal damnation *(Matt. 12:31-32)*. Many believe that blaspheme of the Holy Spirit is the only unpardonable sin. But let us evaluate Scripture to confirm the truth in that assumption **(see also:** Chapter 21 entitled **"Does Sin Prevent Eternal Salvation?")**

B. *What is Blaspheme and Blasphemy of the Holy Spirit?*

According to the Wikipedia dictionary, "Blaspheme" is the act of showing contempt or lack of reverence for God, to religious or holy persons or things, or toward something considered sacred. In relation to blasphemy of the Spirit, blasphemeo or blasfeemía is found in the Biblical Scripture in *(Matt. 12:30-32; Mark 3:28-29; Luke 12:10).* The word blasphemy is derived from the Greek blasphemeo, which means to revile or speak impiously about divine things or having a lack of reverence for God. When the term is directed at a person, it means to hurt someone's reputation by smiting them with evil or slanderous words. It is more than just cursing at another or verbally abusing them, and it generally comes from one's anger. Blasphemeo is speaking deliberate slander about someone with self-serving motives.[32]

The word blasphemeo is from a compound word blásphemos that means to be abusive and insult another's good name. It is a compound of two root words "blapto" and "pheme." Blapto is a primary verb meaning to hinder or injure. Pheme is from a root word "phemi" and means a saying rumor, and phemi originates from phos and phaino, which means to speak. A precise definition of blasphemy in the New Testament:

- *BLASPHEMY – To speak slanderous in an attempt to ruin the good name and reputation of someone else in order to hinder them.*

   To blaspheme the Holy Spirit is to make one's thoughts known in a calculated and deliberately evil way in order to harm Him. It is an attempt to destroy God's reputation and His credibility. It is an effort to hinder God's operations, display lack of reverence for Him, and slander His authority. Satan enjoys persuading believers to think that they have in some past time blasphemed the Holy Ghost. He wants Christians to feel hopeless and in despair so that they begin to question their salvation. Just remember that we are saved by faith, so remain strong in allegiance to God.[3]

Chapter 17

SALVATION GENERATES HOLINESS

Sanctification involves the separation of the believers from the world by Christ after we are justified. It also includes the development into holiness in the believer's Christian life before the rapture. The rapture is not a Biblical term that one can find in their KJV of the Holy Bible. One can find the term referenced in the Catholic Latin Vulgate version of the Bible. The Latin Vulgate contains the word "Rapiemur." "Rapiemur" is the proper tense of the word "Rapio," which is our English word "Rapt" and "Rapture," and it comes from the past participle of "Rapio." Non-Catholic Christians often use the term "Rapture" as a theological term that is used to refer to Biblical end-time prophecy, where believers are caught up in the air to meet with Jesus *(1 Thess. 4:16-17).*[23&39]

Many believers consider this era to be the end-time period, and they expect the rapture to take place sometime in the near future. Jesus will come in the air and the Church (the bride of Christ), or the body of Christ, will be caught up in the air from the earth. Jesus will come with a shout and the voice of an archangel and with the trump of God, and the dead in Christ shall rise first. Then the living believers on earth shall be caught up together with them in the clouds. Believers will be changed into God's perfect likeness (i.e. to be holy, sanctified, and free from sin). We will eternally be with the Lord *(1 Thess. 4:13-18).* The rapture or process of being caught up in the air with Jesus begins our glorification stage.[39]

Many believe that the rapture and glorification process will occur before the 3½ years of tribulation and the 3½ years of great tribulation. Regardless of whether Jesus returns for the Church before, during, or after the start of the tribulation, this should not be the primary focus. Jesus commands us to WATCH for end-times signs and PRAY that we will be accounted worthy to escape end-times tribulations that shall come to pass and to stand before the Son of man *(Luke 21:36).* However, we should concentrate our focus on spreading the Good News of Christ so that we are ready to face the Lord upon His return.[39]

While spreading the Gospel, Christians must simultaneously work towards holiness. Note that the Hebrew Old Testament "pursuit of holiness" differs from and the Greek manner. The Hebrew word for "holy" is "qodesh" and means sacred or dedicated (ceremonially or morally). The Hebrew word for "sanctify" is "qadash" and means to make, pronounce, or observe as holy or clean (ceremonially or morally), to dedicate, appoint, consecrate, keep, prepare, or purify. Under the Law of the Old Covenant, if something was not holy like God, it needed to be made holy through sacrifices. The Temple and its furnishings were considered to be holy. The High Priests of the Temple were ceremonially dedicated, cleansed, and appointed to the office. They were also believed to be holy like God is holy. The tabernacle High Priest foreshadowed Jesus, the Christ. The **high priest** offered a sin offering for the sins of the entire congregation and himself *(Lev. 4:3-21)*.[39]

In the Greek New Testament/Covenant, the word "holy" has a slightly different meaning. One is made holy through Jesus instead of the animal sacrificial sin offering of the High Priest. Paul explained how Jesus became our blameless holy living sacrifice. The word "holy" now has a slightly different meaning of sacred, pure, and blameless, because of how it is accomplished through Christ. To be holy is to be like Christ. *Rom. 11:16* teaches us how we become holy. Paul tells us that if the first fruit is holy, the lump is also holy, and if the root is holy, so are the branches. Paul is referring to what is said by Jesus in *John 15:4-5 (Abide in me, and I in you. As the branch cannot bear fruit of itself, except it abide in the vine (the root); no more can ye, except ye abide in me. I am the vine (the root), you are the branches: He that abides in me, and I in him, the same brings forth much fruit: for without me, you can do nothing).* So if we are in Christ, who is the vine or the root, then we shall become holy like Him.[21,23,&39]

Again, as a result of our God-given free-will, holiness is a decision that requires actions, which follow our decisions. Faith without works is dead *(James 2:20, 2:26)*. Believers must have a desire to be holy like Jesus and become more and more holy as God sanctifies us.

The question of whether or not **holiness** or "death to sin" is necessary in order to receive salvation is one of the most controversial issues amongst both those in the body of Christ, as well as those who have not accepted Jesus as Lord. Contentious conversations sometimes arise as a result of the confusion regarding this topic. Personal, traditional, and philosophical beliefs often add confusion in deliberations concerning keeping oneself saved by holiness or omission of sin. The answer is in the true and pure Word of God. So, let us investigate this subject using the Holy Bible as our source. First, consider why Jesus left a flawless heaven to come to a world that is full of sin or depravity *(John 6:38)*.

A. Why Did Jesus Come from Heaven To Earth?

According to the Book of Isaiah, approximately one year preceding the birth of Jesus, it was prophesied that God would send us a Savior *(Isa. 7:14)*. Jesus testified that He came in order to save the people, which were lost *(Luke 19:10; Matt. 18:11)*. He did not give His life for those who do not need redemption.

The word "redeemer" means to free from the consequences of sin. Considering the definition of redemption, it can be concluded that those that do not, have not, and will not ever sin, would NOT have a need for redemption. According to *Isa. 44:6*, Jesus is our redeemer and died for sinners. Hence, if we are sinless, then we do not need Jesus to redeem us. Unfortunately, we are all born into sin with impure flesh that cannot enter heaven. Consequently, we all need to be redeemed by Jesus.[39]

Re•demp•tion \ri-"demp-sh€n\ *n* : the act of redeeming : the state of being redeemed — **re•demp•tive** \-tiv\ *adj* — **re•demp•to•ry** \-t€-rÈ\ *adj* **re•deem** \ri-"dÈm\ *vb* [ME XXXeedmen, modif. Of MF *redimer,* fr. L *redimere,* fr. *Re-, red-* re- + *emere* to take, buy] **1** : to recover (property) by discharging an obligation **2** : to ransom, free, or rescue by paying a price **3 : to free from the consequences of sin 4 :** to remove the obligation of by payment <the government ~*s* savings bonds>; *also* : to convert into something of value **5** : to make good (a promise) by performing : FULFILL **6** : to atone for — **re•deem•able** *adj* — **re•deem•er** *n*

B. What Is Needed For Eternal Salvation?

Salvation is a gift from God that is offered to all. *(Isa. 45:22 - Look unto me, and be ye saved, all the ends of the earth: for I am God, and there is none else.)*. However, few are chosen to live with God eternally *(Matt. 22:14 - For many are called, but few are chosen)*. Since salvation is a gift, it cannot be bought by the receiver *(Eph. 2:8)*. A gift is something given and requires no payment or purchase from the recipient. The gift of salvation is offered to all that repent and *shalt confess with thy mouth the Lord Jesus, and shalt believe in thine heart that God hath raised him from the dead (Rom. 10:9-10; Luke 13:3-5)*.

Does this mean that those who confess Jesus and believe in His resurrection might be saved? Or does it mean that a person may only be saved if they never sin again? God's Word says that believers **will** be saved, and His Word shall not return to Him void. *Mark 16:16* informs us that by simply believing and being baptized, thou can be saved. On the other hand, he that believeth not will be damned. Through faith, one can confess Jesus as Lord. Faith is belief and trust in God; it is the substance of things hoped for, and the evidence of things not seen *(Heb. 11:1)*. Faith comes by way of the Holy Spirit.[39]

C. If Salvation Is A Gift, Can The Gift Be Retrieved?

Accepting Jesus as Lord means that one is willing to attempt to live according to the will of God versus the will of their flesh. The flesh will continually be tempted to sin. However, the Holy Spirit that dwells within believers gives us the strength to resist the temptation of evil. Accepting Jesus as Lord also involves being submissive unto the Word of God that warns us to repent *(Luke 13:3).* God's will is that man not sin, but God knew that even the elect would sin.

For this reason, from the foundation of the world, God planned a way to redeem us. We have victory over sin because Jesus, who knew no sin, was made to be sin on our behalf *(2 Cor. 5:21).* All human beings have sinned, and if we say that we have not sinned, we make God a liar *(1 John 1:8),* and His word is not in us *(Isa. 53:6 – All we like sheep have gone astray; we have turned every one to his own way; and the LORD hath laid on him the iniquity of us all).*[39]

If or when we do sin against God, we must be honest and open with God. We must admit our sins through confession to God and turn from our sins with the dedication to amend our lives *(1 John 2:1).* Scripture indicates that instead of retrieval of the gift of salvation, Jesus pleads a case for all who have confessed/repented of their sins. God's forgiveness is given through confessing and repentance, and we can be cleansed from all unrighteous *(1 John 1:9).*

One that displays through their actions or words, an irreverence of the Holy Spirit, gets no forgiveness and is in danger of the second death, which is when man's spirit is separated from God's Spirit. Undergoing the second death means that someone spends eternity in the lake of fire where there is everlasting torment in a place where worms do not die and the fire will never be quenched. Remember that according to the Bible, blasphemy of the Holy Spirit is an unforgivable sin. However, restraining from blasphemy of the Holy Spirit does not guarantee heavenly eternal life.[32&39]

D. *Assurance of Our Salvation*

We can be assured of our salvation in the following ways:

1. By realizing that our salvation is a work of God. Believers do not remain saved based on our ability to hold onto God, but His willingness to hold onto us *(Phil. 1:6 - Being confident of this very thing, that he which hath begun a good work in you will perform it until the day of Jesus Christ).*

2. Do you find yourself with the desire to do right? *(1 John 2:29 – If ye know that he is righteous, ye know that every one that doeth righteousness is born of him).*

3. Do you love others? *(1 John 3: 14 - We know that we have passed from death unto life, because we love the brethren)*.

4. Do you have the fruits of the Spirit in your life rather than the works of the flesh? *(Gal. 5:22-23 - But the fruit of the Spirit is love, joy, peace, longsuffering, gentleness, goodness, faith, meekness, temperance)*.

5. With the infilling of the Holy Spirit, you should find an increasing inner conviction that God is true, that the Bible is true, and that your faith is true. The Holy Spirit illumines and instructs the mind, warms the heart to love, and strengthens man's goodwill *(Rom. 8:16 – The Spirit itself beareth witness with our spirit, that we are the children of God)*. The Holy Spirit also inspires believers to loyally submit to God, to worship God, to pray, and to inspire others to serve God.

6. Are you corrected with punishment or suffering by God? Are you disciplined of God? God shapes believers to become more Godly, which is sometimes accomplished through trials, tribulations, or chastising *(Heb. 12:7-8 – If ye endure chastening, God dealeth with you as with sons; for what son is he whom the father chasteneth not? But if ye be without chastisement, whereof all are partakers, then are ye bastards, and not sons)*.

7. Have you often found yourself concerned with the spiritual well-being of others? This is a "Christ-like" characteristic, and to be a Christian is to be Christ-like *(Matt. 12:22-30)*.

8. Scripture confirms that we can be assured of our salvation.

> *1 John 5:13 =* *. . . you that believe on the name of the Son of God; that ye may* ***KNOW*** *that ye have eternal life, and that ye may believe on the name of the Son of God.*

This verse proclaims that we may ***KNOW*** that we are saved. Knowing we are saved means understanding, comprehending, or realizing that we have eternal life.

> *1 Thess. 1:3-4 =* *Remembering without ceasing your work of faith, and labour of love, and patience of hope in our Lord Jesus Christ, in the sight of God and our Father; Knowing, brethren beloved, your election of God.*

E. How Do We Increase Assurance of Our Salvation?

1. Draw nearer to God through prayer *(Heb. 10: 22)*.

2. Study God's word. ***John 1:1*** explains that *"In the beginning was the Word, and the Word was with God, and the Word was God."* Since God is His Word, studying His Word helps us to know God better. Reading God's Word strengthens our relationship with

God and helps us to develop intimacy with Him. It is difficult to build a quality affection or closeness with anyone that we know nothing about.

3. Don't focus on doubts. Some Christians seem to enjoy talking about their doubts just as some people like to talk about their ailments. Doubting comes from a lack of faith and displays uncertainty. It is distrusting or disbelieving. We are saved based on faith, and doubting God is sinful. It can also cause our brothers to stagger. God desires victorious, happy, confident followers *(Heb. 11:6)*.

4. Live your faith. God is honored when you ask big things of Him for the building and the benefit of His kingdom. So, expect His support with abundant faith. *(Matt. 21:21-22; 1 Sam 14:6, 17:37; Dan. 3:17)*.

God has said that His grace is sufficient for us, meaning His grace is capable of satisfying our needs. *(Eph. 2:4-5 - But God, who is rich in mercy, for his great love wherewith he loved us, even when we were dead in sins, hath quickened us together with Christ, by grace ye are saved)*. The strength of God is made perfect in our weakness. Hence, through Him, we are made strong *(2 Cor. 12:9 - And he said unto me, My grace is sufficient for thee: for my strength is made perfect in weakness. Most gladly therefore will I rather glory in my infirmities, that the power of Christ may rest upon me)*.

God rewards good deeds and punishes sin *(Eccles. 4:9)*. However, our good deeds do not pay our way into the Kingdom of God. Only the death of Jesus gives us a second chance to be atoned or reconciled back unto the Father eternally *(Eph. 2:8)*. God weighs the heart and distinguishes between those that are sorrowful for sin, versus those who are in rebellion to Him, and those who worship other things, people, or spirits.[33&39] God knows who only intends to resolve their fear of the unknown eternal lake of fire. They are not willing to truly submit to God or resist their fleshly desires. This rebelliousness prevents the new creature from emerging to cause behavioral changes in the person's lifestyle *(2 Cor. 5:17 - Therefore if any man be in Christ, he is a new creature: old things are passed away; behold, all things are become new)*. This is one of the primary reasons for so many controversial discussions with regard to the topic of one needing to be dead to sin for salvation.

If one is not honest in their confession of Jesus to be given all power and authority over their lives because they only desire salvation, then they have not truly accepted Jesus before man and shall be denied by Jesus before the Father *(Matt. 10:33 - But whosoever shall deny me before men, him will I also deny before my Father which is in heaven)*.[39]

Chapter 18

CHRISTIAN SPIRITUAL GROWTH

Spiritual growth is advancement with one's spiritual maturity. Remember, the soul consists of one's mind, their will, and their emotions. So, spiritual maturity also includes emotional and mental maturity. Spiritual development is a process of maturing from spiritual infancy to adulthood. During this process, one's worldly secular mentality decreases, while their holiness increases through various Christian disciplines, practices, and obedience. Christian practices promote personal reformation, preparation, prayer, praise, profession, and promise.[40]

Believers must be able to regularly examine themselves so that they may confess/repent and be delivered from their iniquity. One may consider keeping a spiritual journal to monitor and document their spiritual growth. Prayer gives the believer time to develop their relationship with God through conversation with Him. In prayer, one can seek direction, give thanks, and commune. Deep meditation prayers in solitude should become a part of one's Christian lifestyle, as well as short, frequent prayers that can be incorporated into one's life in any environment. Even in public, one can pray silently without others being aware of their communication with God. As we grow spiritually, prayer becomes a natural habit.[40]

Praise aids us in our spiritual growth and includes singing, worshipping, and fellowshipping. It is good to praise in private, as well as when we assemble with other believers. We must praise God in both good times and through times of tribulation. Confession of sin aids us in our efforts to grow spiritually. We can confess our faults to one another and pray for one another that we may be spiritually healed and delivered from our sin *(James 5:16)*. The more we grow spiritually, the more we begin to confess of transgressions against God, and the less we attempt to justify or deny our wrongdoings. Our spiritual development continues during the sanctification process of our Christian journey as we await glorification.[40]

Spiritual growth is essential. Humans are born physically and mentally immature. Everyone expects and assumes that, in time, a baby will grow and develop. If the baby fails to grow mentally or physically, there is something wrong with the baby. Similarly, when a person accepts Jesus as Lord, they are considered a born-again babe in Christ. If the born-again babe in Christ fails to mature spiritually, there is something wrong with the babe. If there is no spiritual growth, then the babe should examine their heart to determine whether or not their heart was sincere when their mouth confessed Jesus as their Lord. Spiritual growth is an improvement while working toward spiritual goals. The believer should strive for spiritual maturity or Godliness. As the individual believers mature, the entire church congregation matures.

Scripture encourages the spiritual growth of believers. *Eph. 4:14, 15* instructs us to be no longer children but grow up in Christ. *2 Pet. 3:18* teaches us to grow in the grace and knowledge of Christ. We learn in *2 Thess. 1:3* that the Thessalonians grew in their faith. Failure to grow spiritually can result in one returning back to the world. When believers do not grow spiritually, often it is a result of them lacking the desire to grow. Christians should desire spiritual growth *(1 Pet. 2:2 – As newborn babes, desire the sincere milk of the word, that ye may grow thereby).* Some believers like being spiritual babies because there is less responsibility as a Christian. To whom much is given, much is required *(Luke 12:48).* The more one grows spiritually, the more like Christ they are expected to live. Being a babe in Christ is alright for a while, but it must not be our ultimate goal. We must grow up and become productive and useful in the body of Christ for God's glory and the building of His kingdom. Spiritual growth is needed in order that we may serve the Lord better.[40]

Believers must repent, which leads to spiritual growth and accomplishing our God-given purpose. Some that once wanted to grow lose the aspiration for spiritual development. They seemed to start off with a yearning for the Lord and then lost the longing. They develop apathy or a spirit of negligence. Others became stagnate, get complacent, and think that continual spiritual growth is not needed. Contrarily, God's Word informs us that spiritual growth is continually necessary.

The "Parable of the Sower" (also called the "Parable of the Soils") is a parable of Jesus that is found in the three Synoptic Gospels *(Matt. 13:1-23; Mark 4:1-20; Luke 8:4-15).* A parable is a simple story used to illustrate a moral or spiritual lesson, as told by Jesus in the Gospels. In the parable of the sower, a sower sows seed indiscriminately. Some seed falls on the path (wayside) with no soil, some on rocky ground with little soil, and some on soil that contained thorns. In these cases, the seed is taken away or fails to produce a crop, but when it falls on good soil, it is multiplied, yielding thirty, sixty, or a hundredfold. Our spiritual growth can be compared to how much the seed is multiplied in this parable, and the seed is thought to be the Word of God. When we hear the Gospel, the Word of God (the seed) falls on our hearts. We decide what type of soil our hearts will be like. Will God's seed fall on the path? Will God's seed fall on rocky soil? Will

God's seed fall on thorny soil? Or will God's seed fall on good soil? The answer to these questions determines the magnitude of our spiritual growth.

Jesus explains more thoroughly that the seed represents God's Word, the sower being anyone who professes God's Word, and the various soils represent people's responses to it. The first three types of soil represent a rejection of God's Word, while the last represents acceptance of it (the good soil).

Some of the central things that contribute to one's spiritual growth include:

1. Vision - You must have a vision of your God-given purpose.

2. Listening – Be careful of who and what you listen to. Listen to your spirit man, which requires being still. Don't be led by the flesh. Meditate on God's Word *(Psalm 119:148)*. Listen to a more Godly higher wisdom than your own.

3. Choosing expansion over contraction and being led by the Holy Spirit. Taking action even in the face of fear.

4. Continue building your faith. Do not let defeat destroy your faith.

5. Serve God by assisting Him in the building of His kingdom. Also, provide service to God's children. One must learn to serve before they can lead.

6. Serve your fellow brothers and sisters in Christ.
    Even Jesus served. He washed the feet of the
    disciples *(Matt. 26:14-39; John 13:1-17)*.

Do not take your spiritual growth for granted by placing too much confidence in the flesh *(Phil. 3:3)*. Peter thought that he had reached a spiritual level that would prevent him from denying Jesus. He put too much confidence in his flesh. As a result, he denied Jesus three times in one night *(Matt. 26:31-35)*. Christians will be capable of sin throughout the spiritual growth process until we are glorified. If a believer thinks that they have lived without sin, he is lying to himself and should know that all liars shall have their part in the lake of fire, which is the second death *(Rev. 21:8)*.

*1 Cor. 10:12 = Wherefore let him that thinketh he
standeth take heed lest he fall.*

For those who desire to grow spiritually and are willing to grow, they must do the things that promote growth. Children can physically grow properly when they are fed properly. Likewise, Christians can spiritually grow properly when they are fed properly. Believers don't grow spiritually without feeding on God's Word. As newborn babes in Christ, believers must desire the pure milk of God's Word so that they can mature *(1 Pet. 2:2)*. Believers must grow in the knowledge of Christ because man shall not live by bread alone

(2 Pet. 3:18; Matt. 4:4). We gain knowledge of God's Word through our independent studies, group Bible studies, church services, etc. Some Christians did not study and have been rebuked for not growing as they should have. Other members went back to the world or became spiritual midgets because they do not feed off of God's Word *(Heb. 5:11-14).* We should meditate on the Scripture day and night because learning God's Word is required for spiritual growth *(Psalm 1:1-2; Josh. 1:8).*[40]

You may have heard the saying "practice makes perfect". Well, the truth is that although practice may not always result in perfection, it usually results in improvement. Practice combined with exercise is needed for spiritual growth. We must exercise ourselves toward Godliness by applying Bible principles to our lives *(1 Tim. 4:7).* By studying the Bible continuously, we get a better understanding of God and what He desires of us. Through God's Word, we learn how to minister to others and serve God in a way that is pleasing to Him.

Like physical growth, spiritual growth occurs over time. We can't expect to reach our spiritual goals in an instant. We learn in the Book of James that in order to become perfect and mature, we must have patience *(James 1:4).* Even a common lifestyle may fill one's schedule if we allowed it to, but we must take the time to study and develop spiritually. We are all blessed to have twenty-four hours each day, so not having enough time for God, is a poor excuse. Prioritizing God is essential. God must be the most important entity in your life. Seek first the Kingdom of God and His righteousness, and He will add other things to your account *(Matt. 6:33)*. Making time for God may require sacrificing something on your agenda. Prioritize the items on your schedule. Start eliminating things that require time and do NOT glorify God or please Him. Once one starts doing so, it is amazing how their schedule begins to open up.

On the other hand, do not be anxious for spiritual growth *(Phil. 4:6)*. We are all imperfect and can't expect instant total sanctification. Be patient with God's timing. While spiritual growth is important, it is also important to be patient. Patience is considered to be one of the nine fruits of the Spirit. According to *Gal. 5:22-23,* the fruit of the Spirit includes love, joy, peace, longsuffering, gentleness, goodness, faith, meekness, and temperance. (Note that patience is called longsuffering in the KJV of the Holy Bible). All of the various fruits of the Spirit contribute to our spiritual growth. Moreover, patience is a virtue and God commands us to develop it *(James 5:7)*.

So, have patience, not only regarding the spiritual development of one's self but also maintain patience concerning the spiritual growth of others. It is easy to get impatient with others, but since God is enduring with us, we must be longsuffering with others.

During our spiritual growth process, we may make mistakes. When we were children learning to walk for the first time, we may have fallen repeatedly before mastering the art of walking. Why then would one think that they will learn to walk in Christ perfectly without practice? God will assist us in our development. He corrects, instructs, and punishes us when we sin. Many of the great Bible characters were guilty of iniquity against God and were rebuked. David committed adultery with Bathsheba and was rebuked by Nathan. Apostles forsook Jesus when He was arrested and crucified. Great servants are not people that are sinless. They sin and learn from their mistakes. People are destroyed by their failure to repent of their sins (not because of their sin – see *Prov. 29:1*).

Saul/Paul persecuted Christians before his conversion. Nonetheless, after his transformation from Saul to Paul, he stated that he had wronged or offended no man *(Acts 25:8)*. It was his old man that persecuted believers, and the sin nature of the old man passed away. Paul became a new creature. Like Paul, believers are cleansed from unrighteousness and our sins are cast into the sea of forgetfulness *(Micah 7:19)*. Because of God's compassion for us, we can be justified, sanctified, and glorified.

Chapter 19

WHOLE ARMOR OF GOD – PRAYER TYPES

When someone starts their Christian journey, they are expected to mature in the Lord in many ways *(Eph. 4:12-13).* The Holy Spirit that dwells within believers creates a new creature in that believer. The believer becomes more and more Christ-like. We are warned by God's Word not to remain like spiritual babes. Instead, we are to become sons and daughters of God.[40]

When cultivating our spirituality, we should put on the "Whole Armor of God." Put on God's armor in order to triumph against the devil's schemes.[40] In order to resist or stand against evil, we should put on a protective covering of God. According to *Eph. 6:13–18*, the whole armor of God consists of the following:

1. Girt or fasten on your loins, which are organs of reproduction, with the truth (meaning honesty, the

real state of things, the real events of facts, actuality, correctness, veracity, verity, or agreement with reality).

2. Wear the breastplate of righteousness. Armor your breast by acting on or be in accordance with what is just.

3. Shod your feet with the preparation of the Gospel of peace. The Gospel of peace is the Good News of a state of calmness or public security under God's law. This allows freedom from disturbing thoughts or emotions without aggression.

4. Take the shield of faith to protect from the fiery darts of the wicked. Believe and trust that God guards us against what opposing evil forces bring our way.

5. Take the helmet of salvation. Confessing Jesus as Lord and believing that God raised Him from the dead gives us a protective covering for our heads. The head is the front or upper part of the body that is our chief sense organ. The head is the higher portion, which is safeguarded when we acknowledge our salvation.

6. Take the sword of the Spirit. The sword or the Word of God gives us the capability to cut or thrust.

The Word of God can be used as a defensive mechanism against demonic forces.

7. Pray without ceasing *(1 Thess. 5:17).* Praying always with all prayer and supplication in the Spirit and watching with all perseverance, and asking earnestly and humbly on the behalf of all saints (beseeching). Putting on the whole armor of God includes "Praying all prayers with solicitation or petition."

Christians praying always with **all prayers** involves praying the various types of prayers that are mentioned below:[40]

- Prayers of **petition** (asking prayers).
- Prayers of **consecration** (to induct, as a bishop, into an office with religious rite or to make/declare sacred, or to devote solemnly to a purpose).
- Prayers of **commitment (**to pledge or assign to some particular course or use).
- Prayers of **worship** (giving reverence to god).
- Prayers of **agreement** (two or more having harmony in opinion or action).
- Prayers of **unity** (quantity for a combination of quantities taken as one).

- Prayers of **multiplied prayer power** (*Duet. 32:30*, power is multiplied by 10's of thousands for each additional person that is added to those that pray).

- Prayers of **binding and loosing** *(Matt. 16:19).*

- Prayers of **travailing** (laborious effort or long fatiguing labor, painful work or exertions).

- Praying **in the Spirit** *(Act 19:6; Mark 1:8; 1 Cor. 14:2)* – praying through the Holy Spirit in a tongue or language that is unknown to all men, praying through the Holy Spirit in a tongue or language that is unknown to the person speaking [e.g. a person who has never learned the Aramaic language begins to pray/prophecy/speak in Aramaic by the power of the Holy Spirit], or praying with groaning deep moans *(Rom. 8:26)*.

The Holy Bible gives an indication that prayer is extremely important as we grow spiritually and develop our relationship with the almighty God, our Father. When one of the twelve disciples had the opportunity to put in a face-to-face request, he did not ask Jesus to teach him how to raise the dead, open the eyes of the blind, make the lame walk, or to turn water into wine as Jesus did before witnesses. According to *Luke 11:1,* he requested that Jesus teach them how to pray, and Jesus explained how to pray. Know that it is good to pray

with thanksgiving *(Phil. 14:6)*. Nehemiah displays an
excellent example of how to pray when he wanted the walls of
Jerusalem rebuilt. The prayer method that Nehemiah used
remarkably resembled the manner that Jesus taught. Because
of Nehemiah's prayer, God supplied the resources to rebuild
the walls of Jerusalem in fifty-two days *(Neh. 1)*. Nehemiah's
prayer included seven essential ingredients as indicated below:

1. Nehemiah's prayer began with **"Giving God
   Reverence"** *(Neh. 1:4-5)*. He gave honor and respect
   to God as he specified who specifically he was praying
   to (i.e. the God of heaven, the great and terrible/fearful
   God). Reverencing God should be done with both
   words and behavior. Approach God in right standing
   and in obedience while showing respect and honor to
   Him. Don't blatantly be in disobedience to God's will.

2. Nehemiah **"Made His Request Known"** (*Neh. 1:6* –
   ask God to hear the request). Ask for what you need
   God to do. Note that it is not necessary to instruct God
   on how to do it.

3. Nehemiah **"Confessed Sin"** *(Neh. 1:6)* – Acknowledge
   your sins honestly. It is good to confess/repent of the
   sins of your father, nation, forefathers, and yourself.
   The confessions of your forefather's sins break
   generational curses. If we say that we have no sin, we
   are not honest *(1 John 1:8)*.

4. Nehemiah **"Repeated God's Word Back To Him"** *(Neh. 1:8–9).* Repeat God's Word that He commanded. Reiterate God's promises, which He is faithful and just to uphold.

5. Nehemiah **"Related His Prayer To God's Kingdom"** *(Neh. 1:9).* This was done because God is establishing His kingdom and His eternal plan. Don't focus on establishing your own kingdom (that would be the desire of the flesh). Rather exalt and glorify God's name through your life for the overall scheme of His kingdom.

6. Nehemiah **"Related His Prayer To Redemption"** *(Neh. 1:10).* Redemption means to be bought with a price (which is the blood of Jesus). Jesus paid the price to free us from the consequence of sin or eternal damnation. We were purchased by the blood of Jesus. Hence, go to God in prayer on the basis that we were redeemed by Christ.

7. Nehemiah "**Related His Prayer To The Character Of God**." Reflect on the character of God in your prayer. Nehemiah acknowledged God as being a God of prosperity and mercy *(Neh. 1:11).* Other examples, such as the following, could be vocalized:

    i.   Jehovah Jireh – God is a provider.

    ii. Jehovah Rafa – God is a healer.

iii. Jehovah Shalone – God of peace.

iv. Jehovah M'kaddesh – God that sanctifies *(Lev. 20:7–8)*.

v. Adonai – God which is the master.

vi. El Shaddai – God of blessings and all-sufficiency.

vii. Elohim – all-powerful God of might, creativity, and sovereignty.

Evidence of one's spiritual immaturity includes them being unfamiliar with the Word of God, displaying envy, strife, division, carnality, and having a preoccupation with earthly things, etc. On the other hand, signs of spiritual maturity are noticed by the fruit of the Spirit, spiritual stability, their faith in God, and their desire to be nourished with spiritual food. Jesus is our spiritual food, true Manna from Heaven, Bread of Life, and Living Water.

Believers feed on Christ through the fellowship of the Body of Christ when God's Word is taught. We also learn about God through each another and through the communion of His body and blood *(1 Cor. 10:16-17)*. Repetitive neglect of Scripture, communion, or prayer, is a disregard for Christ Himself. We must meditate on Scripture because it is in God's Word that we find His promises, will, work, rebuke, and knowledge of His being. Recurring prayer and meditation of

Scripture are two of the most important contributing factors in one's personal spiritual growth.

"Devout Solitude" is refraining from interacting with others to be alone with God. This should involve time in silence. "Devout Silence" is not speaking in a quiet place in order to allow us to focus on God's presence. "Devout Fasting" is going without food (or abstinence of something else) for a period of time with a spiritual purpose. This time should include intense prayer. Unless you are participating in a corporate type of fast, consider fasting privately and let God reward you openly.[40]

Acknowledge the Sabbath, where you do no work and rest in God. Pray to God with others during this time. Secrecy is not making our good deeds or qualities known to men. Find sufficiency in God. Remain submissive under God's authority, wisdom, and power. Practice honesty, give love, and allow others to love you. Trust the Holy Spirit that inspired God's Word. Show trust in God. Read His Scriptures regularly, and use them as your guide in life. Worship God with praise acknowledging His greatness and goodness. Pray in conversation with God about your life and others. Develop friendships with those that are disciples' of Christ. Moreover, humbly serve the Lord in all that you do and show compassion to others that are in need.[40]

Chapter 20

WAYS TO EVALUATE SPIRITUAL GROWTH

Christians need to periodically assess their spiritual growth in order to develop their spirituality at a pace that is pleasing to the Lord. This spiritual growth rate can differ from person to person. Know that certain spiritual practices are crucial to building your relationship with God. Christians should routinely study the Bible. Daily reading of the Bible should become as normal as daily eating or drinking. The Word of God is a form of spiritual food, and Jesus is a source of living water that quenches spiritual thirst *(John 4:13-14)*. Do not forsake the assembling of ourselves together so that we may exhort God and one another *(Heb. 10:25)*. The assembling of the body of Christ gives an opportunity for spiritual teaching, fellowship, worship, communion, prayer, and building one another up in faith. Take part in a ministry group, and pray to God daily.

People should question themselves on a consistent basis regarding the above advice. Also, ask yourself, if you are a consumer or a contributor to the Body of Christ. *Heb. 5:12* says that in time a believer ought to become teachers. When they assemble with other believers, they should not just take in. After being given time to learn, one has something to share with others. So they have an obligation to share what they have learned with others. Don't see church only as a place to get spiritually fed. Assemble with efforts to give, as well as receive. Freely receive and freely give *(Matt. 10:8)*. Share the spiritual knowledge that you have received with others. Use your experiences, mistakes, wisdom, knowledge, gifts, success, and failures for the benefit of others.

Ask yourself, if you are spiritually still drinking milk, or have you grown to eat solid foods? Infants drink milk because their body has not developed enough yet to process solid foods. Don't remain a spiritual infant *(Heb. 5:12-14)*. At some point, one should desire an understanding of the deeper and more difficult Christian truths. Do you receive a fresh revelation of the truth on your own? Or do you always depend on your Pastor to spoon feed you? One of the best ways to grow in this area is by absorbing or studying God's Word. Can you discern false teachings if you are taught untruths?

Discernment allows one to distinguish between good and evil. This ability is acquired with spiritual maturity. Is there spiritual growth in your personal relationships? As you grow, others around you should grow as well, if you are sharing what you learn. Do you fully participate in the body of Christ? Do you use your fruit of Spirit and your spiritual gifts for the edification of the church? God blesses us all with varied talents and gifts, which should be used for His glory. Do you have a growing capacity for love? God is love, and if we are growing spiritually, we should develop the ability to be more loving like Him.

We should also gage our selflessness *(Phil. 2:3-8),* and ask ourselves how much we are willing to sacrifice for others? How much are we like Christ, who sacrificed Himself for us? We should become more and more Christ-like every day. Do you serve others as Jesus did? Yielding to God's authority, are you willing to totally and obediently submit your will unto His will? Jesus suffered brutally at the cross. How much will you suffer for the sake of God and His children?

The answers to the above questions tell how successful a person is in their spiritual journey. These questions need to be asked of oneself regularly in order to confirm the progress of the sanctification process.

Chapter 21

DOES SIN PREVENT SALVATION?

Many Christians have spoken of what they call **"The Unpardonable Sin."** Others refer to it as **"The Unforgivable Sin."** They are usually speaking of the blasphemy of the Holy Ghost or Holy Spirit. But is it really unpardonable? Can one inherit the Kingdom of God after they blaspheme the Holy Ghost? We learn how forgiving God is in *Mark 3:28-30*. God promises to forgive all sins including blasphemy (with the exception of blaspheme of the Holy Ghost). Those that blaspheme the Holy Ghost shall not have forgiveness and are in danger of eternal damnation.

> *Mark 3:28-30 = Verily I say unto you, all sins shall be forgiven unto the sons of men, and blasphemies wherewith soever they shall blaspheme: But he that shall blaspheme against the Holy Ghost hath never forgiveness, but is in danger of eternal*

*damnation: Because they said, He hath
an unclean spirit.*

See also: Matt. 12:31-32 and Luke 12:10

Notice that the Scripture does not declare that the person who blasphemes the Holy Ghost will definitely be eternally damned. We can find Biblical examples of where unclean spirits were cast out of people. The Scripture states that the person is "**IN DANGER**" of eternal damnation. According to the Merriam-Webster dictionary, the word "Danger" means that there is a **POSSIBILITY** that one may be hurt or killed. Danger implies that there is a **RISK** or that there is a likelihood of injury, pain, harm, or loss. This means that there is still a slight chance that by God's forgiving grace and mercy, the person who blasphemed the Holy Ghost may still have a chance to repent, be restored by faith in Jesus, and receive eternal life. However, I definitely do NOT advise anyone to take this risk by blaspheming the Holy Ghost. We are not fireproof, so don't play with fire. Let us also notice that the Scripture confirmed that blaspheme of the Holy Ghost will NOT be forgiven.

Suppose you were to blaspheme me personally, and I promised that I would not forgive you, it does not mean that I would NOT let you come to live in my house if you were homeless and needed a place to stay. I do not have to forgive you for blaspheming before I could let you sleep in the spare bedroom of my house. So does God absolutely have to forgive you to allow you to live in His heavenly home? No, because God can do whatever He wants to do (except lie). He would not be a liar if He did so. Remember, God only said that the blasphemer would be in danger of damnation. He did not say that the blasphemer would SURELY be damned as He promised Adam that he would SURELY die upon eating the forbidden fruit. So there is still a small chance that the person could still reach Heaven. I would have to conclude that it is (however unlikely) a chance that one could blaspheme the Holy Ghost, not be forgiven by God for that specific iniquity, and yet still receive eternal life.

Some have called blaspheme of the Holy Ghost, "The **ONLY** Unpardonable Sin." To pardon means to forgive. But again, the question is, does God have to forgive us of ALL SIN in order to allow us to have eternal life? Can a man use his free-will to honestly repent and accept Jesus after blaspheming the Holy Ghost? Based on the Scripture, it is not impossible, but ensuring one's salvation becomes a lot more difficult with the DANGER that blaspheming the Holy Spirit brings.

A. Damnation and the "Mark of the Beast"

According to the Bible, if one takes or accepts the **"Mark of the Beast"** and worships the beast and his image, they shall be damned. *Rev. 14:11* warns us that if someone worships the beast and his image and whosoever receives the mark of his name, shall be put in the lake of fire where the smoke of their torment will ascend up forever and ever.

> **Rev. 19:20** = *And the beast was taken, and with him the false prophet that wrought miracles before him, with which he deceived them that had received the mark of the beast, and them that worshipped his image. These both were cast alive into a lake of fire burning with brimstone.*

During this end-time era, it may get more and more difficult for even some of the believers to resist receiving the mark of the beast. The RFID chip that is already being accepted in today's society fits the description of the Biblical Mark of the Beast. In past generations, accepting the Mark of the Beast was not even an option, because nothing existed that could be used as the Bible describes it. The RFID chips are already being officially used. Eventually, it will be necessary for healthcare, food stamps, housing assistance, and the buying and selling of everything.

It is possible that the mark of the beast might be administered via the RFID chip. Things that make the RFID chip eligible to be used as the beast's mark include:

- The mark of the beast being Biblically described as a physical implant, and the RFID chips can be inserted internally as well. The unholy trinity consists of 1-the antichrist/first beast, 2-the false prophet/second beast, and 3-the dragon/Satan. The second beast of the unholy trinity causes people to worship or reverence the first beast and to receive the mark **"IN"** the person's right hand or inserted **"IN"** their foreheads. Nobody will be able to buy or sell unless they have the mark, or the beast's name, or the number of the beast's name *(Rev. 13:16-18)*. The RFID chip can also be inserted **"IN"** the right hand or **"IN"** the forehead. Everyone may not have hands, but we all have foreheads.

- Furthermore, like the beast's mark, the RFID chip also has the capability of being used in order to prevent society from buying and selling. With a cashless society, an RFID chip can be used for purchases after a collapse of the current currencies.

- The beast's mark will consist of: 1-The mark, 2-The name of the beast, or 3-The "number" of the beast's name (666), which is "the number of man" *(Rev. 13:17)*. The RFID chip can also contain the number "666," as well as the name of the beast.

- The RFID chip is plentiful and affordable enough to be used as the beast's mark. Many people have already purchased chips online for as little as $1.36 each.

Many have had the RFID chips inserted into their pets in order to track their location. Some have even inserted the RFID chip in themselves voluntarily. Chips are currently used in credit cards, passports, driver's licenses, etc. It is not difficult to imagine how the next step could be making it mandatory for the chips to be placed within a person's body.

B. Altering God's Word and Eternal Damnation

God warns man in Biblical Scripture about changing His Word. All Scripture comes from the inspiration of God and is profitable for doctrine, reproof, correction, and instruction for righteousness *(2 Tim. 3:16)*. Humans are not qualified to modify God's Holy infallible Word. For this reason, God warns us that if anyone perverts His Gospel, they will be accursed *(Gal. 1:6-9)*. He also warns us not to alter His Word in *Rev. 22:18-19*.

Rev. 22:18-19 = *For I testify unto every man that heareth the words of the prophecy of this book, If any man shall add unto these things, God shall add unto him the plagues that are written in this book: And if any man shall take away from the words of the book of this prophecy, God shall take away his part out of the book of life, and out of the holy city, and from the things which are written in this book.*

If someone's name is removed from the Book of Life, they will not be saved and will spend eternity in the hellfire. Therefore, removing any of God's Word is a damnable sin.

Chapter 22

THE GREAT WHITE THRONE JUDGMENT
vs.
THE BEMA SEAT JUDGMENT

Scripture informs us that it is appointed unto man once to die and after that **"JUDGMENT"** *(Heb. 9:27)*. After death, there will be two types of judgments, **"The Bema Seat Judgment"** (also known as **"The Judgment Seat of Christ"**) and the **"Great White Throne Judgment."** With this considered, another question arises. If mankind is appointed once to die and after that the judgment, then when do the believers that were LIVING when they were raptured, die? Are they raptured up and then die once they get to heaven?

A. At the Rapture, Do the LIVING Believers Die?

> ***Heb. 9:27 =*** *. . . it is appointed unto men once to die, but after this the judgment:*

Man being "appointed to die" at least once, means that humans are designated with an appointment, to die *(Heb. 9:27)*. Some will be on time for their appointment and die at their appointed time. Some will be late for their appointment and die later than their appointed time.

We know this can occur from the example of Hezekiah *(Isa. 38:5).* Hezekiah prayed and God granted him his desire to extend his life. God extended Hezekiah's life by fifteen years. Furthermore, Enoch and Elijah did not die but were raptured or swept away. However, some believe that they will return to earth as the two end-time prophets/martyrs/witnesses. It is believed by some that they must return to die because they did not die on earth yet. Although Scripture does not specifically tell us who the two end-time witnesses will be, others think that Moses will be one of the two.

Many believe that certain people will miss their appointment to die because of the rapture. They think that the rapture will cause all of the earthly death appointments of the elect to be canceled since they will no longer be here on earth to fulfill their earthly appointments. (This would include things like doctor's appointments, manicure appointments, dentist appointments, and even the appointment of a physical earthly death as a result of the heart failing to beat any longer). All appointments will be canceled for those no longer present on earth.[32&40]

Another explanation involves the fact that many people make the assumption that they know what the word "die" means when they consider the rapture and *Heb. 9:27*. They assume that the word "die" means that someone's heart must stop on earth. Of course, we are not referring to the second death here.

According to Webster's dictionary, the word **"DIE,"** can mean:

a) To pass from physical life. The word pass can mean to move past something or to move through a particular place. This definition rightly describes a living believer being raptured.

b) To **DISAPPEAR** or subside gradually. This definition rightly describes a living believer being raptured even more so.

c) To cease functioning. This definition also rightly describes living believers being raptured.

d) To become indifferent to worldly things. Also, this definition rightly describes living believers being raptured. For after one is raptured, they will not have a need to care for the things of this world.

e) To pass on. This too rightly describes living believers being raptured. The raptured saints will pass on to eternal life.

f) To pass out of existence. In addition, this definition rightly describes living believers being raptured. The raptured saints will pass out of existence on earth.

      g) To stop living. Additionally, this definition
rightly describes living believers being raptured.
The raptured saint will stop living in their
celestial bodies and will receive their glorified
terrestrial bodies.

This study reminded me that Scripture never contradicts
Scripture. If it appears that Scripture is conflicting with other
Scripture, we can be assured that the problem is in our
understanding.[32]

> ***Prov. 4:7*** *= Wisdom is the principal thing; therefore get
> wisdom: and with all thy getting, get
> understanding.*

B. Meaning of "The Bema Seat Judgment" or "The Judgment Seat of Christ"

Rom. 14:10 and ***2 Cor. 5:9*** both speak of the
"Judgment Seat of Christ." Judgment seat is a translation of
one Greek word, "Bema." The word Bema is not actually used
in the KJV Holy Bible. Scripture refers to the judgment seat
of Christ. The bema seat judgment referred to a raised
platform where a Roman magistrate or ruler sat to make
decisions and pass sentence on another ***(Matt. 27:19; John
19:13)***. This event will occur following the resurrection of the
church as described in ***1 Thess. 4:13-18***.[32]

Salvation is a free gift, and there are rewards given to
believers for their faithfulness, as well as the loss of rewards

for a lack of faithfulness. Rewards should not become the major motivating factor for Christians to perform good and Godly works. Some may be bothered by the doctrine of rewards because they see it as focusing on "merit for the believer" rather than "God's grace," and because we should serve the Lord out of love and for God's glory (NOT our own glory).[32]

> ***Rev. 22:12*** = *And, behold, I come quickly; and my reward is with me, to give every man according as his work shall be.*

See also these other significant verses concerning rewards:

> ***Phil. 2:12-13; 1 Cor. 3:11-15, 4:5, 15:10-11; Col. 1:29; Rom. 14:10-11; 2 Cor. 5:9-10; 1 John 2:28; Luke 14:12-14; Rev. 3:11-12, 19:8; 2 Tim. 4:8, and 1 Thess. 4:13-18.***

The order of events related to the Bema Seat Judgment are:

(a) The rapture and receipt of the elect's glorified or resurrected celestial bodies;

(b) Raising/exaltation into the heavens with the Lord;

(c) Examination before the Bema Seat Judgment;

(d) Compensation or rewards at the Bema Seat Judgment.

The Bema Seat judgment will occur somewhere in the heavens in the presence of the Lord. This is discussed in *1 Thess. 4:17* and *Rev. 4:2, 19:8*. Many Pastors and Ministers teach that the participants of the bema seat judgment are

ONLY those saints whose names are written in the Lamb's Book of Life. I was taught this also in seminary. There, we were taught that the Bema Seat Judgment was ONLY for the elect and the Great White Throne Judgment was ONLY for unbelievers. However, *2 Cor. 5:9* teaches: [32]

> *2 Cor. 5:10* = *For we must* **ALL** *appear before the* **JUDGMENT SEAT OF CHRIST**; *that every one may receive the things done in his body, according to that he hath done, whether it be* **GOOD or BAD**.

This is where the controversy occurs. This Scripture gives an indication that the Bema Seat Judgment is for "ALL," both the elect as well as unbelievers. Was this said to believers (meaning ALL believers)? Or, is there a Judgment Seat of Christ at both the Bema Judgment after the rapture and also one at the Great White Throne Judgment that does not take place until the end of the millennium (one-thousand year reign of Christ)?

What we do know for sure is that Jesus Himself will be our examiner or judge at the bema seat judgment. Jesus will bring to light the true nature of our walk and works when we stand before Him at the bema seat judgment *(Rev. 1-2; 1 Cor. 4:5; 2 Cor. 5:10; 1 John 2:28). Rom. 14:10* and *2 Cor. 5:10* call this examination, the "judgment seat of Christ." In other words, Jesus, who is one with God, is our examiner and our rewarder.

Christians will be rewarded based on what they have done for God. This would include rewards for:

a)   Believer's evangelism and aiding the lost with what they need to come to Christ (i.e. providing counsel, prayer for salvation, following up with them, providing people with what they need to help them grow spiritually such as Bibles, transportation to church, clothes for church, etc.)

b)   Tithes

c)   Offerings

d)   Giving to the poor and elderly

e)   Praise and worship

f)   Reading and studying God's Word

g)   Prayer and fasting

h)   Serving church in any way

i)   Etc.

C. Types of the Bema Seat Judgment Rewards [14,18,&31]

o   **The Promise of Crowns** - This may be used as a symbol of victory, authority, and responsibility.

o   **The Promise of Heavenly Treasure - (Matt. 6:20; 1 Pet. 1:4).** They are likely to have eternal value and security.

o   **The Promise of Accolades or Commendations.** Example: "well-done thou good and faithful servant . . ." **(Matt. 25:21; Luke 19:17; 1 Cor. 4:5).**

o   **The Promises to Overcomers.** This could be
rewards of special blessings to those who
overcame special trials *(Rev. 2:7, 2:11, 5, 17,
26)*.

o   **The Promise of Special Responsibilities and
Authority of the Lord's Possessions** *(Matt.
19:28, 24:45-47, 25:21, 23; Luke 19:17-19,
22:29-30; Rev. 2:26).*

D. *Believer's Crowns and Their Significance*[14,18,&31]

*   **The Crown of Thorns -** *(Matt. 27:29; Mark 15:17;
John 19:2, 5).* This is the crown that Christ received
for His work on the cross. It stands for His victory over
sin, Satan, death, and hell.

*   **The Incorruptible Crown -** *(1 Cor. 9:25).*

o   Represents all the crowns, and the differences in
our crowns are also shown.

o   It can also be awarded as a special crown for
faithfulness in running a good race in the earthly
life and exercising self-control in one's service
to the Lord.

*   **The Crown of Exultation or Rejoicing -** *(1 Thess.
2:19; Phil. 4:1).* This crown is a reward that is given
for witnessing and ministry.

- **The Crown of Life** - *(James 1:12; Rev. 2:10)*. This crown is given when a person endures their trials and the temptations that they experience in life.

- **The Crown of Righteousness** - This crown is a reward given for faithfulness in our usage of our gifts. It's rewarded for using the opportunities to serve the Lord and for loving *(2 Tim. 4:8)*.

- **The Crown of Glory** - This crown is a reward promised to Elders for their faithfulness in their responsibilities and for shepherding God's people *(1 Pet. 5:4)*.

- **The Casting of Crowns** - This crown is given because we abide in Christ, and He alone is worthy. We can only be fruitful with His Holy Spirit. This is done by God's grace and not by our goodness *(Rev. 4:10, 11)*.

- **The Many Crowns or Diadems** - This is a crown of royalty and stands for Jesus Christ being King of Kings and Lord of Lords, who has the right to rule and judge *(Rev. 19:12)*.

E. Meaning of "The Great White Throne Judgment"

In the *Book of Revelation*, John shares a prophecy that explains what arises in the end-times. There will come a time when the dead in Christ will rise to meet Jesus in the air *(1

Thess. 4:16-17). After they rise, the believers that remain living on earth shall join them in the air to meet Christ. This catching up in the air is called the "Rapture" or the "First Resurrection." The believers are considered to be the "Body of Christ" or the "Bride of Christ." At the sixth seal, there will be a battle of the "Great Day of the Lord" and a gathering together of armies for the battle of "Armageddon" in "Megiddo, Israel" *(Rev. 16:16)*.

Scripture in ***Revelation*** tells us about the judgments that will take place after the rapture and after the one-thousand year reign of Christ. Sometime after the rapture, the antichrist (the first beast) and the false prophet (the second beast) are thrown into the lake of fire.

The dragon (Satan) is imprisoned in the bottomless pit for the one-thousand year reign of Christ (also called the millennial reign of Christ). Throughout this period, Satan has no ability to deceive the nations. During the one-thousand years, Christ will rule all nations as King on the earth from a New Jerusalem Temple in Israel *(Rev. 20:1-6)*. Once the one-thousand years are completed, Satan must be released for a brief time.

Satan will cause many that live during the millennial to rebel against God, bringing them to a battle that is called "Gog and Magog." God miraculously devours the rebels with a fire that falls down from heaven. Finally, Satan is then thrown into the lake of fire, where the antichrist and the false prophet will be. The three entities of the false trinity will forever be tormented in the lake which burns eternally *(Rev. 20:7-10)*.[36&37]

Afterward, the great white throne judgment will take place with Jesus as the judge. Our heavenly Father does not judge; instead, He leaves the judgment for the Son *(John 5:22)*. The dead unbelievers will be resurrected (called the second resurrection), and they will stand before the throne to be judged based on what is written in the books according to what they had done. Since we are saved by faith through Christ, our works cannot save us. However, sinful works may condemn us *(Rev. 21:8-10; Eph. 5:5; 1 Cor. 6:9-10; Gal. 5:19-21; Col. 3:5-6)*.[36&37]

The Book of Life will be used to display the names of those who will escape the eternal lake of fire. The sea, death, and hades give up the dead in them to be judged. Death and hades will be thrown into the lake of fire, which is the second death. Those who reject Jesus as Lord will inherit the lake of the everlasting fire. *Rev. 20:11-15* makes it clear that The Great White Throne is the final judgment. And many of them that sleep in the dust of the earth will awake (some to shame and everlasting contempt - *Dan. 12:2*). *(*See also*: Rev. 3:21, 20:11-15; Matt. 25:41, 46; 1 Cor. 15:54-55)*. Mercifully, believers are not judged in the Great White Throne Judgment

because their sin has been paid for by Jesus.[32,36,&37]

> ***Rev. 20:11-15*** = *"And I saw a great white throne, and
> him that sat on it, from whose face the earth and
> the heaven fled away; and there was found no
> place for them. And I saw the dead, small and
> great, stand before God; and the books were
> opened: and another book was opened, which is
> [the book] of life: and the dead were judged out of
> those things which were written in the books,
> according to their works. And the sea gave up the
> dead which were in it; and death and hell delivered
> up the dead which were in them: and they were
> judged every man according to their works. And
> death and hell were cast into the lake of fire. This
> is the second death. And whosoever was not found
> written in the book of life was cast into the lake of
> fire".*

Chapter 23

TERMINUS FACTS

If someone confesses Jesus to be their Lord and believes in their heart that God raised Him from the dead, they shall be saved. With the heart, man can have faith in the death, burial, and resurrection of Jesus and become righteousness. With their mouth, they can confess Him as Lord and acquire salvation *(Rom. 10:9-10)*. When someone receives God's free gift of salvation, they are filled or baptized with the Holy Ghost. Hence, after death, believers receive eternal life with God. We learned in *John 3:5* that unless a person is born of water and of the Holy Spirit, he can't enter into God's kingdom. So, in addition to repenting of sins, we must also be born of the Spirit, receiving the infilling of the Holy Ghost.

Acts 2:38 says that Peter preached instructing men to repent and be baptized in the name of Jesus for the remission of their sins. He also taught that they would receive the gift of the Holy Ghost. Receiving the gift of the Holy Ghost is being

born of the Holy Spirit. Everyone should understand the
process of salvation; otherwise, they can end up being
destroyed because of their lack of knowledge *(Hos. 4:6).*

> ***Hos. 4:6*** *= My people are destroyed for lack of
> knowledge: because thou hast rejected knowledge, I
> will also reject thee, that thou shalt be no priest to me:
> seeing thou hast forgotten the law of thy God, I will
> also forget thy children.*

Should anyone reject Christ, they will spend eternity in
the lake of fire and brimstone, which is the second death. By
God's grace and mercy, with faith in the Lord Jesus, we are
justified and reconciled back unto God, the Father. Although
God wishes that none perish, many are called, but few are
chosen *(Matt. 20:16, 22:14).* When we are redeemed, we are
adopted by God as His children, and become joint heirs with
Christ *(Rom. 8:17).* The adoption of the believing Gentiles
means that we are engrafted into the olive tree or engrafted
into Israel. Israel (God serving believers) are God's chosen
people. God chose the lineage of Abraham, Isaac, and Joseph
to bring forth His only begotten son to redeem mankind from
our sin.

Satan tried to kill/destroy the chosen lineage from the
beginning. Yet he failed, and God prevailed. Now, as a result
of Jesus coming to bear our sins on the cross reconciling
believers back to God the Father, Israel consists of believing
Jews and believing Gentiles. And all of Israel shall be saved

(Rom. 11:26). Thanks to Jesus, believing Gentiles will also have an inheritance to the Abrahamic covenant promises. Praise God.

There are various phases of the salvation process that include the following:

STEPS IN OUR SALVATION PLAN:

Jesus Saved Us from Sin	Descr.	By Way Of	Phase Called	Time Frame	Bible Ref.
Penalty Of Sin	Penalty Of Sin Is Death	Christ	Justifi-cation	Past Tense	*Eph. 2:8-9* *Rom. 3:28*
Power Of Sin	Power Of Sin Is The Flesh	Holy Spirit	Sanctifi-cation	Present Tense	*Phil. 2:12* *Heb. 10:28*
Presence Of Sin	Presence Of Sin Is This World & This Body	Life In A New World & New Body	Glorifi-cation	Future Tense	*Rom. 13:11* *1 Cor. 15:42*

Once we accept Jesus as Lord, we are considered babes in Christ and are expected to spiritually mature during our walk with Christ. Salvation should result in our becoming more holy (Christ-like) during our sanctification process.

Many disciplines should be practiced to aid us in our spiritual growth process (e.g. fasting, reading Scripture, worship, prayer, having Christian friends and prayer partners, solitude, silence, Sabbath acknowledgment, secrecy, submission, personal reflection, regular assembling with other believers, service to the Lord, etc.).

We are created by God as free moral agents that have the ability to decide for ourselves which god(s) or God that we will serve. We should spend our lives preparing for the afterlife and getting ready to meet God *(Amos 4:12)*. Judgment Day is coming soon for everyone, and we must be ready for it.

Jesus promised that He would go and prepare a place for us. Heaven is a prepared place for prepared people. We must decide whether we will spend eternity in Heaven or the hellfire. We must understand that neglecting to make a choice is choosing Satan. *Strait is the gate, and narrow is the way, which leads unto life, and few there be that find it (Matt. 7:13-14).* The choice is ours to make. God's Scripture should be the foundation of our theological awareness. We must fear God and keep His commandments *(Eccles. 12:13)*.

If you have not already done so, choose this day who you will serve. I pray that you have been persuaded to choose the Lord Jesus, and inherit eternal life with Christ. If you were already a believer prior to reading this book, I pray that it has encouraged you to rededicate your life to Christ in total submission and obedience, and that the teachings assist you in totally fulfilling your God-given purpose. Lastly, I pray that all who read this will be inspired to shine their light in dark places spreading the Gospel wherever you go.

ABOUT THE AUTHOR
&
ACKNOWLEDGMENTS

I began formal theology/ministry studies at Jericho Christian College, National Bible College & Seminary, and Calvary Christian College, where I was blessed to be taught by some of the world's most amazing Christian professors such as: the late Apostle Betty Peebles, Pastor Joel Peebles, Co-Pastor Yolanda Peebles, Minister Bobby Henry, Elder Linda Pyles, Minister Bessy, Dr. Juliet Onunako, Pastor/Dr. Florida Morehead, Dr. B. E. Short-Clark, Pastor/Dr. Archer, Dr. Wallace, Rev./Dr. Sutherland, Pastor/Dr. Kenneth Brown, Dr. Mark D. Talbert, Dr. Janece Parks, Dr. Samuel Odenyo, Pastor/Dr. Timothy Wood, Dr. John F. Warren, Dr. Mark Roberson, Dr. William Gray, Dr. Jacqueline Rice, Pastor Wanda Sisco, etc.

I must also acknowledge and express special thanks to all of my highly anointed informal instructors that include: Pastor Woodard, Bishop John Chandler, Pastor John K. Jenkins Sr., Pastor John A. Cherry Sr., Minister Michael McFadden, Pastor Jay Cameron, Pastor Deron Cloud, and Pastor/Dr. Mark Thompson.

I express my sincere thanks first to Jehovah (my heavenly Father), Jesus Christ (my redeemer), the Holy Ghost (my keeper), and secondly, to all of the superlative educators that are listed above, to my supportive mother (Bidgie Froe), and to my belated beloved inspiring father (Dana Froe), for their encouragement. I am immensely grateful to them all for aiding me with my educational accomplishments that include the acquisition of the following degrees/diploma: "Doctor of Ministry," "Master of Divinity," "Bachelor of Theology," "Bachelor of Ministry and Christian Counseling," and "Christian Discipleship Diploma."

Additionally, I also dedicate this document to all of those that are listed above, and it is my prayer that they all be blessed to an even greater degree, than that which they have blessed me. And may God get the glory.

BIBLIOGRAPHY - REFERENCE MATERIAL

1. Theopedia Encyclopedia of Biblical Christianity
2. Wikipedia Encyclopedia
3. Zane Publishing Inc. ©, Merriam-Webster Dictionary
4. International Standard Bible Encyclopedia
5. Heaven, Finding our True Home, by Douglass Connelly
6. The Free Dictionary by Farlex (TheFreeDictionary.com)
7. John Gill's Bible Exposition Word Today, by John Gill
8. Matthew Henry Exposition of the Bible by Matthew Henry
9. Bible Hell: Sheol, hades, Tarturus, Gehenna, by Hansen
10. Theodore Beza's supralapsarian predestination, by Beeke, Joel R., 12 no 2 Spring 2003, p 69-84. Publication Type: Journal Article
11. Another look at the infra/sub/supralapsarian debate, by Mouw, Richard J., Calvin Theological Journal, 35 no 1 Apr 2000, p 136-151. Publication Type: Journal Article.
12. Growth of a supralapsarian Christology, by Peter Toon. Source: Evangelical Quarterly Journal, 1967, p 23-29. Publication Type: Journal Article
13. Journal of Religion, 60 no 3 Jl 1980, p 247-271. Publication Type: Journal Article
14. Journal of Theology, 59 no 1 2006, p 27-44, Journal Article
15. Library of Congress Control No.: 04019302, A proof and Explanation of the decree of God, Published by Hartford, Printed by T. Green at the Heart and Crown, 1767
16. The decrees of God and of kings in the Aramaic correspondence of Ezra, by Conklin, Blane, Source: Proceedings – Eastern Great Lake and Midwest Biblical Societies, 2001, p 81-89. Publication Type: Article
17. Three decrees of God from Theban tomb 32, by Llaszio Kakosy. Source: Orientalia Lovaniensia periodica, 23 1992, p 311-328. Publication Type: Article

18. Decrees of God, by Bromiley, Geoffrey William, Source: Christianity Today, April 10, 1961, p 18-19. Publication Type: Article

19. Smith's Bible Dictionary, William Smith, L.L.D., Thomas Nelson Publishers,

20. MS Encarta Encyclopedia © 1994 MS Corp, by Funk

21. Keyed Strong's Vine's complete Expository dictionary, Old & New Test words, by W. Vine, © 1996 1984

22. Nelson's quick reference Bible Dictionary, by W. Smith

23. Strong's Greek Dictionary

24. Zondervan's Compact Bible Dictionary, © 1993

25. The King James Version of the Holy Bible

26. Calvinism: A History by D. G. Hart

27. Holman's Bible Dictionary

28. Easton's Illustrated Dictionary

29. The Doctrine of Justification by Author W. Pink, © 2007

30. Jesus Christ: Source of Salvation by M. Pennock, © 2011

31. Genesis Gap/Pre-Adamic creation, by Lowrance © 2011

32. Soteriology: Historical-Systematic look . . . Doctrine of Salvation-Sanctification, © 2011

33. Fall from Grace, Redeemed by Faith, by Emma Robertson, © 2013

34. The Lake of Fire: who, what, when, where, and why, by Rich Denius © 2011

35. What are Election and Predestination? Basics of Faith, by R. Phillips © 2006

36. God's Foreknowledge-Man's Free-will, by Rice © 2004

37. Woven Together/Grace in Adoption, by Hope © 2013

38. Free Grace Soteriology: Revised by D. Anderson © 2013

39. Sanctification & Glorification, by M. Roberts, © 1997

40. Spiritual Maturity / Spiritual Growth Principles, by J. Sanders © 2007

41. Finney's Systematic Theology, by C. Finney © 2007

42. Zionist Influence on America by Peter Christian